SpringerBriefs in Social Work

SpringerBriefs in Social Work and Social Change

Series Editors
Rajendra Baikady, Department of Social Work & Community Development
University of Johannesburg
Johannesburg, South Africa

Jaroslaw Przeperski, Centre for Family Research
Nicolaus Copernicus University
Torun, Poland

S. M. Sajid, Department of Social Work
Jamia Millia Islamia
New Delhi, India

SpringerBriefs in Social Work and Social Change is a compact book series of authored and edited briefs on the state-of-the-art literature on social work and social change as well as globalization and social change, neoliberalism and social change, and societal response to social change, with special reference to social work education, research and practice.

The principal aim of the Series is to examine social change in a constantly changing world with new economic, political and social orders and how social work as a human service profession responds to these changes. Contributions in this Series go beyond accepting change as an inevitable force and reflect on our power in influencing, redirecting and contemplating social change. It is with this principal aim that we call upon academia, policy-makers, researchers and educators in social work, at all levels of their career stage, to explore the positive part of social change; i.e., what can we learn from social change while revisiting its negativity and impact.

Volumes published in this Series approach social change at different levels of society (whether local, regional, national, transnational, or at the macro, meso and micro levels). The Series identifies and defines the concept of social change within the social work context and its impact on human development at various national and international scopes.

Featuring compact volumes of 50 to 125 pages, *SpringerBriefs in Social Work and Social Change* is a comprehensive collection of high-quality literature on social change, with a primary focus on social work, contributed by educators, researchers, and practitioners across the globe. Both solicited and unsolicited manuscripts are considered for publication in this Series.

More information about this series at https://link.springer.com/bookseries/16748

Maik Arnold

Social Work Leadership and Management

Current Approaches and Concepts for Social and Human Service Organisations

Maik Arnold
Fachhochschule Dresden - University of Applied Sciences
Dresden, Germany

ISSN 2195-3104 ISSN 2195-3112 (electronic)
SpringerBriefs in Social Work
ISSN 2731-0760 ISSN 2731-0779
SpringerBriefs in Social Work and Social Change
ISBN 978-3-031-17631-9 ISBN 978-3-031-17632-6 (eBook)
https://doi.org/10.1007/978-3-031-17632-6

© The Author(s), under exclusive license to Springer Nature Switzerland AG 2022

This work is subject to copyright. All rights are solely and exclusively licensed by the Publisher, whether the whole or part of the material is concerned, specifically the rights of translation, reprinting, reuse of illustrations, recitation, broadcasting, reproduction on microfilms or in any other physical way, and transmission or information storage and retrieval, electronic adaptation, computer software, or by similar or dissimilar methodology now known or hereafter developed.

The use of general descriptive names, registered names, trademarks, service marks, etc. in this publication does not imply, even in the absence of a specific statement, that such names are exempt from the relevant protective laws and regulations and therefore free for general use.

The publisher, the authors, and the editors are safe to assume that the advice and information in this book are believed to be true and accurate at the date of publication. Neither the publisher nor the authors or the editors give a warranty, expressed or implied, with respect to the material contained herein or for any errors or omissions that may have been made. The publisher remains neutral with regard to jurisdictional claims in published maps and institutional affiliations.

This Springer imprint is published by the registered company Springer Nature Switzerland AG
The registered company address is: Gewerbestrasse 11, 6330 Cham, Switzerland

Foreword

The society we live in today experiences several social issues related to structural inequalities, racism, poverty, marginalization, violence, and the climate crisis. In order to strengthen human well-being and achieve the United Nations Sustainable Development Goals (SDGs) by 2030, we need to tackle rising inequality, poverty, and marginalization in different societies across the globe. Social workers in several professional settings continue to face challenges related to delivering adequate welfare provisions to needy people. On the one hand, social service organizations in several countries are struggling to recruit and retain enough well-qualified and skillful social workers in a time when welfare cuts, neoliberal marketization, and privatization of goods and services in several countries are resulting in unprecedented social inequality and disparity. On the other hand, the increasing demand for services and welfare assistance has led to an urgent need for more timely interventions of various human service professionals. Developing knowledgeable, skill-oriented, and ethically competent social workers is, thus, more important today than ever before (Baikady et al., 2022).

In times of neoliberal market economy and welfare cuts, social workers as human service professionals struggle to deliver equal access to welfare provisions for all but especially marginalized and vulnerable populations. Further unprecedented events such as the COVID-19 pandemic, natural disasters resulting from uncontrolled climate change, and violence and war require human service professionals' urgent interventions to rescue, rebuild, and rehabilitate lives in order to ensure social justice, equality, and human dignity. In order to meet the growing demand for skilled and competent human service professionals, social work programs across the globe need to refocus their curriculum and pedagogy by including training and skills development for graduates.

The professional reputation and public perception of social work continue to be low in many countries. In addition, the low pay, increasing caseloads, and lack of public trust are all hindering the social work profession from executing its mandate. Among these challenges, the training and retention of a skilled workforce is the most important one. This phenomenon of increased turnover intentions of social work graduates from active social work or welfare service in several countries has been discussed (Baikady et al., 2021, 2022a; Jiang et al., 2017). Other challenges facing social work is the lack of effective and efficient institutional leadership as well as trained and experienced educators and field supervisors. The need for these professionals in various roles of training social workers and managing their work is especially felt in regions where one experiences lots of violence and threat to human rights and human life.

Maik Arnold in his book, *Social Work Leadership and Management: Current Approaches and Concepts for Social and Human Service Organisations,* examines various aspects of leadership training and management. This book is a valuable source of literature for social welfare organizations and non-profit institutions to train, upskill, and effectively manage their human service workforce. Arnold also focuses on the importance of research on leadership and management of social work in the book. There appears to be little research on and an understanding of what leadership and management qualities social work and other human service professionals need to execute their professional responsibilities effectively and efficiently. There have been proposals for the use of reflexivity training in social work education and practice to enhance learning and practice capabilities (Przeperski & Ciczkowska-Giedziun, 2022).

The changing social order, its accompanying social problems, and the need to redirect social change require new approaches to social work education and practice in contemporary society. Social work as a social change agent needs to prepare its future professionals to be capable of dealing with the changing social realities and societal demands. Social work educational institutions across the globe need to foster newer approaches to education and training. The focus of educational programs at undergraduate and postgraduate levels should be on building capacities and skills required for social change and transformation. This book by Arnold provides a thoughtful examination of social work leadership that is required for the twenty-first century global society. In the five extensively researched chapters, Arnold presents different dimensions and functions of classical and new leadership approaches relevant to social and human service organizations. This book is very timely and contributes to the ongoing debates on integrating leadership components into social work education at various levels of teaching and learning programs (Brilliant, 1986; Rank & Hutchison, 2000).

Leadership development in social work education and practice has been a topic of debate for a long time. However, questions on the type and models of leadership and the type of leadership skills training social work students require to improve their capability to handle the social problems they will have to address have not been adequately researched. Promoting and retaining leaders who can inspire and lead teams of social work students, educators, practitioners, and policy makers to achieve the goals and aims of the profession is very important. In an effort to strengthen social work leadership and capacity building, several local and global professional associations are working on skills and capacity building, knowledge development, production, and sharing among social work educators and agency supervisors at both the national and global levels. Organizations such as the International Association of Schools of Social Work (IASSW), International Federation of Social Workers (IFSW), and the Council on Social Work Education (CSWE), among others, are continuously working towards the enhancement of social work education and practice in different contexts. These collaborative efforts by international organizations are contributing towards the Social Change Model of Leadership (Komives & Wagner, 2009), which particularly aims to develop collaborative leadership in social work to effect social change.

Contemporary society is changing fast, and every society irrespective of their level of economic and technological development is facing social issues. Widening disparity and deteriorating human connections demand for new approaches and methods to deal with human relations and improve well-being. While social work believes in collaboration, partnership, and advocacy as the approach to bring positive social change in any society, the profession also should focus on facilitating more research and international debates on developing, promoting, and sustaining well-thought leadership development modules for social work and social care professionals. In a constantly changing society, fostering excellent social work leadership will be more important than ever, and this book by Maik Arnold kickstarts what we hope is a fruitful debate that leads to everlasting and meaningful change in the field of social work education and practice across the globe.

Jarosław Przeperski
Nicolaus Copernicus University
Warsaw, Poland

Rajendra Baikady
University of Johannesburg
Johannesburg, South Africa
30 July 2022

References

Baikady, R., Nadesan, V., & Gao, J. (2022a). What brings people to the social work classroom: a comparative perspective from India and China. *Social Work Education*, 1–17. https://doi.org/10.1080/02615479.2022.2065257

Baikady, R., Cheng, S. L., & Gao, J. G. (2021b). Serving the state or serving the people? The dilemma of social work graduates in Mainland China. *Critical and Radical Social Work*, 9(2), 219–235. https://doi.org/10.1332/204986021X16114103358825

Baikady, R., Nadesan, V., Sajid, S. M., & Islam, M. R. (2022). Introduction: Signature Pedagogy–A Practice Laboratory of Social Work Education. In *The Routledge Handbook of Field Work Education in Social Work* (pp. 1–10). Routledge.

Brilliant, E. L. (1986). Social work leadership: A missing ingredient? Social Work, 31, 325–331.

Jiang, H., Wang, Y., Chui, E., & Xu, Y. (2017). Professional identity and turnover intentions of social workers in Beijing, China: The roles of job satisfaction and agency type. *International Social Work*, 62(1), 146–160. https://doi.org/10.1177/0020872817712564

Komives, S. R., & Wagner, W. (Eds.). (2009). Leadership for a better world: Understanding the social change model of leadership development. San Francisco, CA: Jossey-Bass.

Przeperski, J., & Ciczkowska-Giedziun, M. (2022). Reflexivity as a Pivotal Component of Fieldwork in Social Work Education. In R. Baikady, S. M. Sajid, V. Nadesan, & M. R. Islam (eds.), *The Routledge Handbook of Field Work Education in Social Work*, 423. Routledge.

Rank, M. G., & Hutchison, W. S. (2000). An analysis of leadership within the social work profession. *Journal of Social Work Education*, 36, 487–502.

"Today, in times of crisis and uncertainty, we are forced to find alternative ways to collaborate, educate, communicate and manage groups and individuals, which requires new thinking about practice, but also leadership and management. In Social Work Leadership and Management: Current Approaches and Concepts for Social and Human Service Organisations, *Maik Arnold provides a good framework for leadership, including new leadership concepts. This book makes an important contribution to social work and human service institutions and beyond. Readers will find theories combined with practices in an engaging way. This is required reading not only for the future leaders, but today's leaders as well."*

—**Karmen Toros**, Tallinn University,
Tallinn, Estonia

Contents

1	**Introduction**		1
	References		3
2	**Theoretical Background and Terminology**		5
	2.1	Leadership vs. Management	5
	2.2	Typology of Leadership Approaches	11
		2.2.1 Classical-Traditional Leadership Approaches and Theories	12
		2.2.2 New Leadership Approaches	19
	References		28
3	**Leadership Research and Its Application to Social Work Practice**		33
	3.1	Dimensions of Leadership	33
	3.2	Leadership as a Context of Interaction and Power	34
	3.3	Systemic-Organisational Leadership Theories	35
	3.4	Adaptive Leadership	37
	3.5	Conclusion	39
	References		40
4	**Transformation of Leadership and Collaboration in Human Service Organisations**		43
	4.1	Context and Framework of New Leadership Concepts	43
	4.2	The Practice of Adaptive Leadership	45
		4.2.1 Situation Challenges	46
		4.2.2 Leadership Behaviour	47
		4.2.3 Adaptive Work	48
		4.2.4 Strengths and Weaknesses of the Model	49
	4.3	Digital Leadership	50
		4.3.1 Digitalisation in Social and Human Services	50
		4.3.2 Leadership in Digital Transformation	51
		4.3.3 Towards a Sustainable Framework for Digital Leadership	52

	4.4	Agile Leadership	56
		4.4.1 Introduction	56
		4.4.2 Agile Leadership in Social Work Organisations	56
		4.4.3 Challenges for the Implementation of Agile Leadership Practices in Social Work Organisations	60
	References	62
5	**Conclusion and Outlook**	65
	5.1	Implications for Leadership and Collaboration in Social Work Organisations	65
	5.2	Requirements for Management Learning and Teaching in Higher Education	66
	5.3	Leadership and Management in Uncertain Times	67
	References	70
Index	73

About the Author

Maik Arnold Dipl.-Kfm., Dr. rer. soc., FRSA, is Professor of Social Work Management and Vice President for Research, Innovation and Transfer at Fachhochschule Dresden – University of Applied Science Dresden, Germany. From 2013 to 2017, he was managing director and research associate at the Centre for Research, Further Education, and Counselling at the University of Applied Sciences for Social Work in Dresden. He has conducted various projects in the fields of intercultural competence and cooperation, game-based learning, digital education, and organisation research; was research associate at the Oxford Centre for Mission Studies (UK); and visiting fellow at the Goethe Institute in Cracow (PL), the Institute for Advanced Study in Humanities in Essen and the Global Young Faculty in Essen (Stiftung Mercator). After his studies in business administration and intercultural communication at the Chemnitz University of Technology (Germany) and the Strathclyde University (Glasgow, UK), as well as Protestant theology at the Evangelical Church of Central Germany, he received his PhD in social sciences from Ruhr-Universität Bochum (Germany) in 2009. Since 2020, he holds the honorary position as a board member of the International Association of Social Work Management (INAS e.V.) and is speaker of the German Network of Scholarship of Teaching and Learning (SoTL). He is a certified systemic coach for change management and an intercultural trainer. He hosts the podcast Managing Around – A Podcast about Management, Culture, and Social Sciences, which is part of the Talk About Organisations Podcast Network. As a published author of various books, textbooks, book chapters, journal articles and presentations locally, nationally and internationally, he specialises in social work management didactics and education, digital education management, management of social organisations, systemic coaching, intercultural communication and competence, cultural psychology, religious identity in intercultural contexts, as well as methodology of qualitative empirical research. His last co-edited book *Leadership and Organisation: New Developments in the Management of the Social and Health Economy* (*Führung und*

Organisation: Neue Entwicklungen im Management der Sozial- und Gesundheitswirtschaft) was published by Springer in 2019, and another edited book *Handbook of Applied Teaching and Learning in Social Work Management Education: Theories, Methods, and Practices in Higher Education* will be published by Springer in 2022. For more information, visit http://www.maik-arnold.de.

List of Figures

Fig. 2.1	Theoretical-conceptual approaches to leadership.	12
Fig. 2.2	Situational leadership by Hersey and Blanchard (1969), as cited in Lippold, 2019, p. 22	17
Fig. 2.3	New leadership approaches.	19
Fig. 4.1	Model of adaptive leadership according to Heifetz (1994)	46
Fig. 4.2	Digital transformation framework.	53
Fig. 4.3	Road map for digital leadership using the example of an educational institution.	55
Fig. 4.4	Scaling of an agile organisation.	57
Fig. 4.5	Process of agile transformation.	61
Fig. 5.1	Hybrid function of social work management education.	68

List of Tables

Table 2.1	Historical comparison between manager and leader characteristics	8
Table 2.2	Distinction between transactional and transformational leadership	14
Table 2.3	Overview on new leadership theories	23
Table 4.1	Stumbling blocks and solutions for agile leadership	61

Chapter 1
Introduction

Both leadership and management are constantly confronted with various challenges that go hand in hand with new forms of education and knowledge work: Employees want to be individually supported. Leaders must be able to act as entrepreneurs. Organisational culture should be developed from a holistic perspective. Leadership within self-organised organisational contexts has increasingly become the focus of attention. In addition, organisations and their employees are struggling with the effects of VUCA or BANI framework conditions (cf. e.g., Mack et al., 2015). *Social Work Leadership and Management: Current Approaches and Concepts for Human Service Institutions* addresses these challenges and aims to describe and discuss the transformation of leadership in the context of selected recent leadership approaches, starting with an overview of classic and recent leadership approaches, also including adaptive, digital and agile leadership. The book casts light on organisational change in this type of institutions and provides new insights into how leadership can be implemented in social economy institutions.

Ultimately, it is also the objective of this book to develop a current literature review through the selection, translation and evaluation of management approaches and concepts relevant to the social economy, which is not directly accomplished by various recent textbooks and handbooks on general business administration and management (e.g. Endres & Weibler, 2019; Iszatt-White & Saunders, 2020; Lippold, 2019; Northouse, 2016). In addition, the approaches to leadership and organisation and the management of social work organisations presented in previous reviews are revisited, differentiated and advanced (e.g. Arnold, 2019; Fröse, 2015; Fröse et al., 2019).

One directly related question concerns the extent to which the approaches presented can help leaders in social enterprises to deal with current challenges in greater depth and develop appropriate answers to questions such as the following: What is leadership? Where does the term come from? How does it differ from the concept of management? What do current leaders need in terms of management and leadership qualifications for long-term and forward-looking management? In answering these questions and for the future shaping of leadership and cooperation in social service organisations, the term "leadership" is chosen as the key concept, when it refers to the research literature as well as the description of the different approaches and traditions.

The book is divided into five chapters. After this introduction (Chap. 1), a clarification of the theoretical foundations and the concept of leadership is provided, distinguishing it from, for example, management (Chap. 2). Additionally, a concise overview of various leadership approaches and theories is provided – both the classic-traditional and the new leadership. The results of a current literature review are presented with reference to the relevant research publications on leadership (Chap. 3). The literature review reveals that the concept of leadership has been developed in many ways in the literature and can be differentiated into a myriad of dimensions and functions. In addition, various theoretical strands of historical traditions and schools can be derived from the research literature, which can be laid across the classical and more recent leadership approaches described in the second section: leadership as an interaction and power context, leadership in a systemic-organisational context and in the context of adaptive leadership approaches and in particular leadership with crucial importance for the management of social work organisations. In Chap. 4, two leadership approaches are presented in detail particularly relevant for the design of leadership and cooperation in social work and human service organisations: adaptive leadership and digital leadership. The book concludes with Chap. 5 and a discussion of implications for leadership practice and training of future leaders in social and human services as well as an outlook based on the presented leadership approaches and concepts.

Finally, a note on the source material for this book: While the content of this book is related to the author's previous research underlying leadership and management, not only the theoretical background in Chap. 2 but also the findings from a systematic review of literature on leadership approaches in Chap. 3 have been expanded to include a detailed analysis and discussion of their current implications for social work and human service institutions (cf. Arnold, 2017, 2019, 2022; Fröse et al., 2019). Additionally, in Chap. 4, the author's previous research about leading change through the practice of adaptive leadership (cf. Arnold, 2019), digital leadership in hybrid organisations (Arnold, 2020, 2021) and the challenges for implementing agile leadership principles in social work institutions (cf. Arnold, 2022) has been included and expanded to present a status quo prevalent in recent literature.

Acknowledgement Several people were involved in the creation of this book, without whose assistance the work would not have been completed in such a short time. I would like to sincerely thank Dr. Bettina North who twisted and turned every comma, syntax and word in order to give this work a consistent gown.

References

Arnold, M. (2017). Diakonische Praxis und ihre Gestaltung in Organisationen. In M. Arnold, D. Bonchino-Demmler, R. Evers, M. Hussmann, & U. Liedke (Eds.), *Perspektiven diakonischer Profilentwicklung: Ein Arbeitsbuch am Beispiel von Einrichtungen der Diakonie in Sachsen* (pp. 28–48). EVA.

Arnold, M. (2019). Leading change in human service Organisations in the 21st century. In M. W. Fröse, B. Naake, & M. Arnold (Eds.), *Führung und Organisation: Neue Entwicklungen im Management der Sozial- und Gesundheitswirtschaft* (pp. 159–174). Springer. https://doi.org/10.1007/978-3-658-24193-3_8

Arnold, M. (2020). Leading digital change – Management of hybridity and change in education and social service institutions. In T. Koehler, E. Schoop, & N. Kahnwald (Eds.), Gemeinschaften in Neuen Medien. *Von hybriden Realitäten zu hybriden Gemeinschaften. Proceedings of 23nd Conference GeNeMe 2020* (pp. 332–341). TUD Press. https://nbn-resolving.org/urn:nbn:de:bsz:14-qucosa2-741338

Arnold, M. (2021). Leading digital change and the management of hybridity in social work organizations. In F. Özsungur (Ed.), *Handbook of research on policies, protocols, and practices for social work in the digital world* (pp. 55–73). IGI Global. https://doi.org/10.4018/978-1-7998-7772-1.ch004

Arnold, M. (2022). Agiles Führen und Managen in der Sozialen Arbeit: Stolpersteine auf dem Weg zur agilen Führungspraxis. In J. Grothe (Ed.), *Leitung, Führung und Management in der Sozialen Arbeit: Bedeutungshorizonte und Konzepte auf dem Prüfstand* (pp. 123–138). Beltz Juventa.

Endres, S., & Weibler, J. (2019). *Plural Leadership: Eine zukunftsweisende Alternative zur One-Man-Show*. Springer. https://doi.org/10.1007/978-3-658-27116-9

Fröse, M. (2015). Transformationen in ›sozialen‹ Organisationen: Verborgene Komplexitäten. *Ein Entwurf*. Würzburg: Ergon.

Fröse, M. W., Naake, B., & Arnold, M. (2019). Quo Vadis – Leadership und organisation. In M. W. Fröse, B. Naake, & M. Arnold (Eds.), *Führung und Organisation: Neue Entwicklungen im Management der Sozial- und Gesundheitswirtschaft* (pp. 1–30). Springer. https://doi.org/10.1007/978-3-658-24193-3_1

Iszatt-White, M., & Saunders, C. (2020). *Leadership*. Oxford University Press.

Lippold, D. (2019). *Führungskultur im Wandel: Klassische und moderne Führungsansätze im Zeitalter der Digitalisierung*. Springer Gabler. https://doi.org/10.1007/978-3-658-25855-9

Mack, O., Khare, A., Krämer, A., & Burgartz, T. (Eds.). (2015). *Managing in a VUCA world*. Springer. https://doi.org/10.1007/978-3-319-16889-0

Northouse, P. G. (2016). Leadership: Theory and practice. In *Leadership theory and practice* (7th ed.). Sage.

Chapter 2
Theoretical Background and Terminology

2.1 Leadership vs. Management[1]

When dealing with the topic of human resource management in social work institutions, differentiating between the terms leadership and management is inevitable. While used interchangeably, both terms have developed in different contexts (cf. for an overview Eck, 2007; Goethals et al., 2004; Kotterman, 2006; Neuberger, 2002). Zaleznik (1977) and Kotter (1990b) introduced a differentiation in the usage of these terms to the discussion. Zaleznik's (1977) seminal study acknowledges that an organisations' success requires both effective managers and successful leaders, but also contents that those managers and leaders contribute differently to the development of an organisation. Accordingly, different kinds of professionals are needed: managers who advocate for stability, assert authority and work to fulfil goals vs. leaders who are responsible for immediate change or innovations and who can emphatically secure people's commitment. More recently, Kotter (1990a, p. 85) stated that:

> Leadership is different from management, but not for the reason most people think. Leadership isn't mystical and mysterious. It has nothing to do with having 'charisma' or other exotic personality traits. It's not the province of a chosen few. Nor is leadership necessarily better than management or a replacement for it. Rather, leadership and management are two distinctive and complementary activities. Both are necessary for success in an increasingly complex and volatile business environment.

The use of the terms goes back to a long conceptual history and different academic traditions, as well as diverse discourses in practice (Bass & Bass, 2009). We will

---

[1] The outlined summary of the current state of research on the development of leadership is based on a literature review by Fröse et al. (2019). On the one hand, essential lines of development are summarised, and, on the other hand, an expansion, refinement and differentiation are carried out on the basis of more recent research findings.

© The Author(s), under exclusive license to Springer Nature Switzerland AG 2022
M. Arnold, *Social Work Leadership and Management*, SpringerBriefs in Social Work, https://doi.org/10.1007/978-3-031-17632-6_2

begin by looking at the traditional and (post)modern approaches to leadership research before introducing the term management in its fairly modern conception.

As Northouse (2016) points out, there is a wide range of theoretical approaches dealing with the question of how leadership can be understood, ranging from a processual view (e.g. Bass, 1990a; Bryman, 1992; Bryman et al., 2011; Day & Antonakis, 2012; Gardner, 2011; Hickman, 2009; Mumford, 2006; Rost, 1991) to the conceptualisation of personality dispositions and communication theory approaches (e.g. Barge, 1994; Fairhurst, 2011; Tourish & Jackson, 2008, among others), to relational theories (e.g. Uhl-Bien et al., 2012). In any case, leadership is a multidimensional construct, and, as already observed by Stogdill (1974, p. 7) in his still topical literature review, far more definitions than authors can be identified as early as the 1980s. According to Steinle (1978, p. 27), leadership is:

> understood as a systematically structured process of influencing the realisation of intended performance results; leadership is thus in essence goal-oriented and future-related guidance of action, whereby this influence is directed towards performance and satisfaction.

In his analysis, Rost (1991) documented more than 200 different conceptualisations in the period from 1900 to 1990 (cf. also Neuberger, 2002, who identified more than 130 definitions of leadership). In the 1920s, leadership was still understood as a leader's ability to impose their will on those being led, with values and behaviours such as subordination, respect, loyalty and willingness to cooperate (Moore, 1927, p. 124, as cited in Northouse, 2016, p. 2). For an insight into the diverse evolution of that term, the following excerpts from classic leadership research will serve as an example, which later allow for a summarised characterisation of the term:

- *Leadership is always connected with the achievement of common goals:* "the behaviour of an individual [...] directing the activities of a group towards a shared goal" (Hemphill & Coons, 1957, p. 7).
- *Leadership, culture change and change management in organisations are directly linked*: "the ability to step outside the culture [...] to start evolutionary change processes that are more adaptive" (Schein, 1992, p. 2).
- *Leadership is closely linked to the relationship between leaders and followers*: "The only definition of a leader is someone who has followers. To gain followers requires influence but does not exclude the lack of integrity in achieving this" (Drucker, 2013, p. 103).
- *Leadership must communicate visions, foster trust and develop their potential for action*: "Leadership is a function of knowing yourself, having a vision that is well communicated, building trust among colleagues, and taking effective action to realise your own leadership potential" (Bennis et al., 2001).

The same applies to the term "management", which has also experienced different interpretations depending on the context and situation. The root of "management" can be derived from *lat. manus* (the hand) and *manu agere* (to act with the hand). Management means "bringing something together" or "leading by the hand" or "working with the hand". Thus, management is about manual activities, to produce, make or guide something and to perform final activities. In the narrower

2.1 Leadership vs. Management

sense, it means something like working and directing with the bare hands. In the original meaning of the term, management is therefore "active work", and in the broader sense, it is connected with a certain artistry. This is demonstrated precisely by the fact that a competent person knows and can implement all necessary steps for planning, implementing and controlling a process.

According to the Oxford English Dictionary (2022), "to manage" generally means "to control or be in charge of a business, a team, an organisation, land, etc." This ability is demonstrated, for example, by being responsible for or managing an institution or a certain activity/area. Similarly, the basic meaning of this term can be summarised as follows (Oxford English Dictionary, 2022): "succeed in doing something, especially something difficult" and "to succeed in achieving or producing something". In other words, it is about achieving, creating or accomplishing something even in difficult circumstances. This last aspect underlines the importance of management, which is a task relevant to existence ("surviving") and generally serves survival: "to be able to live or survive without having much money, support, sleep, etc." (Oxford English Dictionary, 2022). Thus, management cannot be reduced to the often cited economic contexts alone: In the British context, management mainly means "to direct/be in control of", emphasising the activity of directing, guiding and reviewing objectives to be achieved. This was initially related to the administrative role of management. In the US context, the related term "executives" is more commonly used. In a corporate context, for example, one speaks of executive management, the board of directors. A chief executive officer (CEO), for example, is the head of the board of directors who represents the organisation internally and externally. In this parlance, management has always been understood as the "science of administration" (the scientific consideration of the design and management of organisations) (Hendry, 2013, p. 1).

Neuberger (2002) summarises this conceptual horizon of the classical concept of management in such a way that management in the broader sense stands for organising things. This complex activity and competence includes, in particular, operationalising contexts, acting in different situations and contexts, differentiating between alternatives, hierarchising and prioritising (sub-)tasks, establishing and relating contexts, typifying events, giving meaning through narratives as well as integrating different management tasks and theorising, modelling and analysing structures, processes and decisions (Neuberger, 2002, pp. 15–30, as cited in Fröse, 2015, pp. 254–257). The term management is used in this context to refer to the implementation of goal-oriented activities or tasks that are guided by economic principles, which serve to manage, control and shape organisations. This can include various functions, areas and institutions (e.g. planning, leadership processes, staff development, organisation-related management).

The frequently quoted formulaic differentiation between leadership and management by Warren Bennis (1998, p. 47), "Managers do the things right, leaders do the right thing", falls short from today's perspective (later also in Birch, 1999). As shown in Table 2.1, different authors made similar distinctions between management and leadership.

Table 2.1 Historical comparison between manager and leader characteristics

Leader characteristics	Manager characteristics
Zaleznik (1977)	
Focus on people	Focus on system and structure
Has followers	Has subordinates
Informal influence	Formal authority
Takes risk	Minimize risks
Facilitates decisions	Makes decisions
Doing the right things	Doing things right
Long-range perspective	Short-range perspective
Transformational	Transactional
Sets strategies and vision	Plans and budgets
Challenges	Maintains
Values	Rules
Innovation	Standardization
Bennis (1989)	
Innovates, creative	Administers
An original	A copy
Develops	Maintains
Focuses on people	Focuses on systems and structure
Inspires trust	Relies on control
Long-range perspective	Short-range view
Asks what and why	Asks how and when
Eye on the horizon	Eye on the bottom line
Originates	Imitates
Challenges the status quo	Accepts the status quo
Own person	Classic good soldier
Does the right thing	Does things right
Chapman (1989)	
Advance their operations	Protect their operations
Seek responsibility	Accept responsibility
Take calculated risks	Minimize risks
Generate speaking opportunities	Accept speaking opportunities
Set "unreasonable" goals	Set reasonable goals
Challenge problem employees	Pacify problem employees
Strive for an exciting working environment	Strive for a comfortable working environment
Use power forcefully	Use power cautiously
Delegate enthusiastically	Delegate cautiously
View workers as potential followers	View workers as employees
Certo (1997)	
Soul	Mind
Visionary	Rational
Passionate	Consulting
Creative	Persistent

(continued)

2.1 Leadership vs. Management

Table 2.1 (continued)

Leader characteristics	Manager characteristics
Flexible	Problem-solving
Inspiring	Tough-minded
Innovative	Analytical
Courageous	Structured
Imaginative	Deliberate
Experimental	Authoritative
Independent	Stabilizing
Bennis and Goldsmith (1997)	
Innovates	Administers
An original	A copy
Develops	Maintains
Investigates reality	Accepts reality
Focuses on people	Focuses on systems
Inspires trust	Relies on control
Has a long-range perspective	Has a short-range view
Asks what and why	Asks how and when
Has his or her eye on the horizon	Has his or her eye always on the bottom line
Originates	Imitates
Challenges the status quo	Accepts the status quo
His or her own person	The classic good soldier
Counselling, empowerment	Counselling, empowerment
Manager, work with a mechanistic approach	Manager, work with a mechanistic approach
Buchanan and Huczynski, 2019; *based on* **Kotter** (1990b)	
Establishing directions: Vision of the future, develop strategies	Plans and budgets: Decide action plans and timetables
Aligning people: Communicate vision and strategy	Organizing and staffing: Decide structure and allocate staff
Motivating and inspiring: Energize people to overcome obstacles	Controlling, problem-solving: Monitor results against plan
Produces positive and sometimes dramatic change	Produces order, consistency and predictability
Rigotti (1994, p. 58ff.) cited in **Fröse** (2015, p. 256)	
dux	rex
(Army) leader	King, regent, ruler
To lead, to precede	To lead, to shape, to dominate
Archetype: Romulus (First King of Rome)	Archetype: Numa (Second King of Rome)
Indo-European deity: Varuna (attributes: attacking, dark, enthusiastic, violent, warlike, unpredictable, frenetic, magical, demanding)	Indo-European deity: Mithra (attributes: rational, clear, calm, benevolent, control those being led, liberal, just)
Guiding maxim: battle	Guiding maxim: harmony
Guiding metaphor: war	Guiding metaphor: ship of state, building of state

(continued)

Table 2.1 (continued)

Leader characteristics	Manager characteristics
Goals: gaining power, overthrow, change, dynamics, conflict	Goals: maintaining power, securing power, continuity, statics, order, security
Political concept: Machiavelli	Political concept: Aristotle
Political theory: conservatism, Marxism, imperialism, romanticism, "realism"	Political theory: humanism, liberalism, utilitarianism
The Other: (potential) enemy	The other: (potential) friend
Northouse (2016, **p.14**)	
Establishing direction	Planning and budgeting
Create a vision	Establish agendas
Clarify big picture	Set timetables
Set strategies	Allocate resources
Aligning people	Organizing and staffing
Communicate goals	Provide structure
Seek commitment	Make job placements
Build teams and coalitions	Establish rules and procedures
Motivating and inspiring	Controlling and problem-solving
Inspire and energize	Develop incentives
Empower followers	Generate creative solutions
Satisfy unmet needs	Take corrective action
Lunenburg (2011)	
Focuses on people	Focuses on things
Looks outward	Looks inwards
Articulates a vision	Executes plans
Creates the future	Improves the present
Sees the forest	Sees the trees
Empowers	Controls
Colleagues	Subordinates
Trusts and develops	Directs and coordinates
Does the right things	Does things right
Creates change	Manages change
Serves subordinates	Serves superordinates
Uses influence	Uses authority
Uses conflict	Avoids conflict
Acts decisively	Acts responsibly

Extended and adapted from Algahtani (2014, pp. 78–80), Rigotti (1994, pp. 58–60), Northouse (2016, p.14)

This discussion about the semantics of managers and leaders suggests that these are at least analytically and dialectically separable areas of responsibility. Rather, however, it can be assumed that different ways of thinking are anticipated here, depending on whether one ascribes or receives the "label" as manager or leader. Neuberger (2002) even argues for excluding the administrative/managerial component entirely from the concept of leadership, which must be accompanied by processes of de-bureaucratisation and de-routinisation:

The 'new leadership approach' of charismatic and transformational leadership urges 'finally lead again'! The routines of technical or bureaucratic managing and administering are to be filled with spirit and life, which can only be imparted by rousing visionary leaders. (Neuberger, 2002, p. VII, as cited in Fröse, 2015, p. 255, transl. MA)

This confrontation is problematic not only because it juxtaposes two mutually related and occasionally overlapping types of leadership but also because it makes strong judgements based on one-dimensional attributions that are all too often equated with ambivalent historical personalities. Nevertheless, this distinction is still based on a trait-oriented leadership approach (cf. Sect. 2.2.1.1). Zaleznik (1977) had already pointed out in his differentiation between manager and leader:

> Managers and leaders are two different animals. Leaders, like artists, tolerate chaos and lack of structure. They keep answers in suspense, preventing premature closure on important issues. Managers seek order, control, and rapid resolution of problems. (p. 67)

In the historical-systematic analysis by Burns (1978), a similar power-theoretical classification of "leadership and followership" can be found:

> Leadership over human beings is exercised when persons with certain motives and purposes mobilize, in competition or conflict with others, their own institutional, political, psychological and other resources in such a manner as to arouse, engage, and satisfy the motives of followers. (Burns, 1978, p. 273)

Hinterhuber (2009, p. 22) pointed to a stronger connection and integration of leadership and management: Every manager should also fulfil a leadership function by identifying the needs of employees and customers, and by trying to meet these in the best possible way. Leadership is also linked to the managerial personality, their expertise as well as their capacity for action. The term "leadership" and not "management" is mainly used hereafter to establish consistency with the predominantly referenced linguistic literature while avoiding an incomplete and inadequate translation of leadership into, for example, "management".

2.2 Typology of Leadership Approaches

The concept of leadership is a multidimensional construct that has been shaped by various leadership theories and methods, including their respective concepts of human nature (*Menschenbild*). A distinction can be made between the classical-traditional and new leadership approaches, which operate in different reference systems (von Au, 2016, p. 6, Northouse, 2016). The *classical-traditional leadership approaches and theories* mainly focus on one-, two- or multidimensional relationships, while the *new leadership approaches* take also into account several other factors from institutional, political, technological and legal contexts, their relationship to individual and group behaviour as well as dynamic-situational, systemic and cultural influences on leadership. A brief overview of selected approaches is provided in the next two subsections.

2.2.1 Classical-Traditional Leadership Approaches and Theories

Classical leadership theories refer to individual factors of leadership, which can be differentiated between trait, behavioural and situational approaches (cf. e.g. Lippold, 2019, pp. 2–22; Northouse, 2016, pp. 19–114; von Au, 2016, pp. 6–13; for an overview, see Fig. 2.1).

In this book, we examine leadership as a multifaceted concept. Building on the research literature, the following three subsections will introduce the reader to various classical approaches to leadership that may be applied to enhance leadership in social organisations and social work settings.

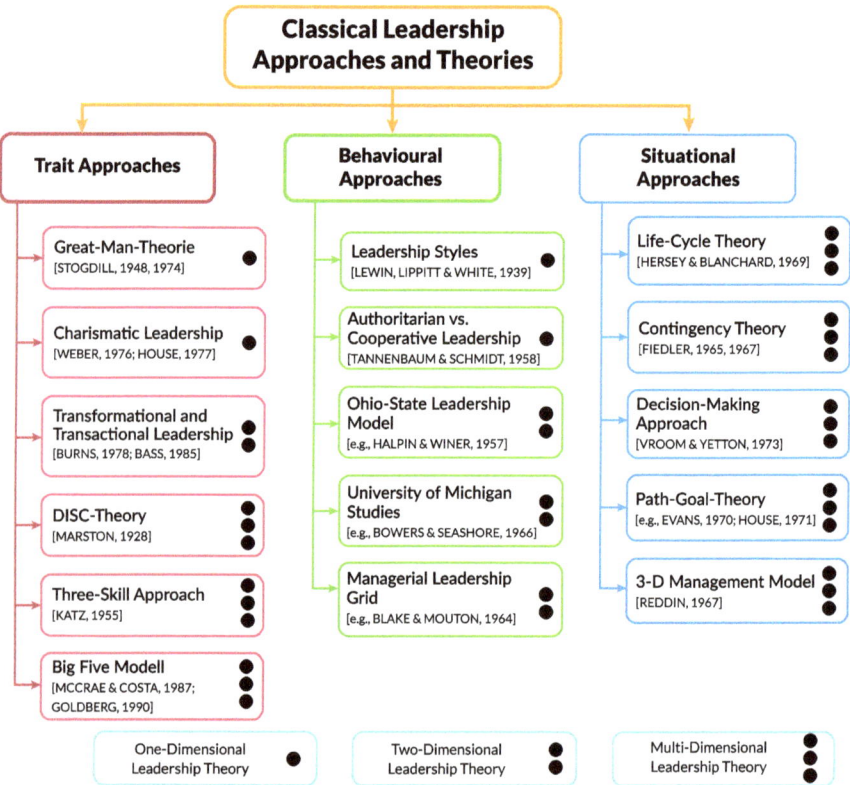

Fig. 2.1 Theoretical-conceptual approaches to leadership. (Extended and adapted from Lippold, 2019, p. 5. Adapted and translated by permission from Springer Nature: *Klassische Führungsansätze und -theorien*. In: *Führungskultur im Wandel* by Dirk Lippold. © 2019 Springer Fachmedien Wiesbaden GmbH, part of Springer Nature; Northouse, 2016; author's translation)

2.2.1.1 Person-Centred and Trait-Oriented Approaches

In person-centred *trait theory* leadership approaches, the focus lies particularly on personality traits. These include, for example, the seminal *great man theory* (Stogdill, 1948/1974) and *charismatic leadership* (House, 1977; Weber, 1976) but also *skills theory* (Katz, 1955) and the *five-factor model (big five)* (Goldberg, 1990; McCrae & Costa, 1987). All these approaches have in common that leadership is approached from the perspective of the manager. According to the *great man theory*, leaders are perceived in terms of their innate abilities and character traits, which they can bring into everyday leadership. This approach is highly theoretical and lacks plausible empirical evidence. According to *trait theory*, leaders possess "certain time-stable and situation-independent traits that enable them to exert influence over the actions of those they lead" (von Au, 2016, p. 8, transl. MA). "It was believed that people were born with these traits, and that only the 'great' people possessed them" (Northouse, 2016, p. 19). Similarly, also the charismatic leadership theory has received great attention so far, which assumes that a manager's charisma has a significant impact on the behaviour of the staff they oversee. The most widely used theory in trait-based leadership research is the internationally extensively researched five-factor model (e.g. John et al., 2008). According to this model, the five main dimensions of a person's personality include (1) neuroticism versus emotional stability, (2) hostility versus agreeableness, (3) lack of goal setting versus conscientiousness, (4) introversion versus extraversion and (5) closed-mindedness versus openness to new experiences (von Au, 2016, p. 8, transl. MA). Various studies have shown that extraversion and emotional stability, for example, have a particular influence on leadership behaviour. It may be critically questioned, however, whether it is appropriate to describe leadership success on the basis of individual personality while assuming cross-cultural or universal character traits (e.g. Judge et al., 2002). Finally, the *DISC model* assumes that a leader's behavioural patterns are governed by their personality structure. The personality structure (personality profile) of a leader is determined by which of the four personality qualities: dominance (active force to overcome resistance in the environment), inducement (use of charm to overcome obstacles), submission (a sincere and deliberate acknowledgement of the need of fulfilling a request) and compliance (fearful acclimatisation to a greater power) (adapted from Marston, 1928).

In contrast, the *skills theory* captures those personality traits that are not innate but have been acquired or learned over the course of life (Northouse, 2016, pp. 43–60). Similar to the trait theory, the skills theory focuses on person-centred characteristics of leaders. The two most prominent theoretical approaches in this context are the *three-skills approach* according to Robert Katz (1955), which distinguishes between technical, human and conceptual skills (see also Northouse, 2016, pp. 44–45), and the *competency model* according to Mumford and colleagues (Mumford, 2006; Mumford et al., 2000), which differentiates between individual attributes (e.g. general cognitive ability, crystallised cognitive ability, motivation, personality), competencies (e.g. problem-solving skills, social judgement skills and knowledge) and leadership outcomes (effective problem-solving, performance)

(Mumford et al., 2000, p. 23). Katz's approach initially laid the groundwork for conceptualising leadership in terms of basic skills and abilities in the mid-1950s, but was eventually rediscovered in the mid-1990s as part of the empirically based competency approaches (Northouse, 2016, pp. 46–47). Although Mumford and colleagues already differentiate cognitive abilities, motivation and personality variables as factors of leadership, the latter approach can generally be assigned to personality-oriented leadership theories (Northouse, 2016, p. 60).

Furthermore, Burns (1978) and Bass (1985, 1990b) mark a distinction between *transactional and transformational leadership*: Transactional leadership includes all reciprocal leadership styles that work with motivational reinforcement effects. Based on the fulfilment of expected performance, there is a corresponding reward for the services rendered, which in turn should lead to an increase in performance. This leadership approach is most likely to be internalised in target agreements. In contrast, transformational leadership focuses on the charisma of the leader, on inspiring those being led through a vision, on understanding their needs and on increasing their commitment (cf. also Table 2.2).

Recent empirical research in the field of management and leadership in social work organisations (Arnold et al., 2017, pp. 260–261) has shown that the trait theory is still part of management discourses. Fröse (2015, pp. 316–321) defines three degrees of leadership expertise. The first set of *metacognitive skills* leaders should possess are hermeneutic, interpersonal, reflective and interpretive abilities. In the second set, they should also show *personal governance*, such as introspective self-evaluation, ethical management and self-analysis as well as moral leadership. This highlights the fact that people in social work organisations need to build and reflect not only their personal but also their *professional identity*. Finally, leadership requires an understanding of concepts of human nature and organisations (Morgan, 1986).

Table 2.2 Distinction between transactional and transformational leadership

Facets of leadership characteristics	Transactional leadership	Transformational leadership
Coordinating mechanism of leadership	Contracts	Excitement
	Rewards	Social connection
	Punishment	Trust
		Creativity
Aim of employee motivation	Extrinsic motivation	Intrinsic motivation
Focus of target achievement	Rather short-term	Medium- and long-term
Contents of the motivation	Material aims	Ideal aims
Individual role of the leader	Instructor	Teacher
		Coach

Stock-Homburg, 2013, p. 464, as cited in Lippold, 2019, p. 8. Adapted and translated by permission from Springer Nature: *Klassische Führungsansätze und -theorien*. In: *Führungskultur im Wandel* by Dirk Lippold. © 2019 Springer Fachmedien Wiesbaden GmbH, as part of Springer Nature; author's translation

2.2.1.2 Behavioural Approaches

Behavioural leadership approaches, in contrast to trait theories, focus on the actions and perspectives of leaders. The *leadership style approach* (Northouse, 2016, pp. 71–82; von Au, 2016, p. 7) has produced a wide range of single- to multidimensional leadership constructs. The best known in this field is probably the one-dimensional leadership style theory of Kurt Lewin et al. (1939), which distinguishes between democratic, laissez-faire and authoritative leadership styles. This approach was later expanded, for example, in the Tannenbaum and Schmidt (1973) continuum of seven leadership styles between the poles of authoritarian and cooperative leadership – supplemented in between by the patriarchal, advisory, consultative and participatory and delegating leadership styles. "Authoritarian behaviour is characterised by the fact that the manager assigns tasks to the employees, prescribes the way in which the tasks are to be carried out and does not show personal appreciation to the employees" (Lippold, 2019, pp. 11–12, transl. MA). In the cooperative style, the manager's cooperative behaviour encourages workers to self-distribute job duties and discuss tasks and goals in groups. The leader respects all group members and actively participates in group activities. In general, this type of leadership style approaches assume that a "democratic leadership style [promotes; MA] job satisfaction and positive attitudes of workers while an authoritarian style of the superior reduces both" (von Au, 2016, p. 9, transl. MA). A critical view of Lewin's leadership style approach is that the results of his experiments (with children, among others) were "inadmissibly generalised" and simply transferred to other contexts and phases of personality development (adulthood) (Brose & Hentzel, 1990, p. 103).

Also included in this category of leadership theorems is the two-dimensional *Ohio State University leadership model* of the late 1940s based on the findings of Stogdill's (1948) research, which distinguishes between person orientation and task orientation as the two factors influencing leadership behaviour (e.g. Halpin & Winer, 1957; Hemphill & Coons, 1957). In various scientific studies in the 1960s, for example, it was examined how the behaviour of employees towards their superiors changes with regard to the two dimensions of person orientation and task orientation. While person orientation is understood, for example, as the extent to which the manager supports, involves, praises and acknowledges their employees, task orientation, on the contrary, focuses on the development of a goal, the planning and coordination of action and the organisation of the management process (von Au, 2016, pp. 9–10). Similarly, researchers further explored leadership behaviour, focusing primarily on the influence of leadership on the performance of smaller groups in the *University of Michigan studies* (Bowers & Seashore, 1966, among others). Two types of leadership were distinguished: employee orientation and production orientation representing two ends of a continuum. In the course of these studies, three essential factors of effective leadership were identified: task-oriented, relationship-oriented and participation-oriented behaviour, which was later also taken up in various situational approaches (cf. Sect. 2.2.1.3).

Based on the two-dimensional Ohio State University approach, among other things, the so-called *managerial grid approach* was later developed in the 1960s by Blake and Mouton (1964) and is widely used in organisational training and development. In the behavioural grid, the "person-oriented leadership behaviour with socio-emotional aspects" (concern for people to achieve goals) is represented on the vertical and the "task-oriented leadership behaviour with factual-rational aspects" (concern for production to achieve organisational tasks) on the horizontal (von Au, 2016, p. 10; transl. MA). In Reddin's *3-D management style theory* (1967), this grid is supplemented by a third dimension, the effectiveness of the leadership style, and greater consideration is given to the organisation-related framework conditions.

While behavioural approaches focus on acquired, learned or adopted leadership skills, it is critical to note that these studies do not adequately show how leadership behaviour is linked to leadership success (Bryman, 1992). In this context, Yukl (1994, p. 75) points out that "results from this massive research effort have been mostly contradictory and inconclusive". Furthermore, the original aim of the above-mentioned approaches to describe a universally valid leadership style that could be effective in (almost) any situation must be criticised as a failure (Northouse, 2016, p. 81). Finally, the approaches are also accompanied by the perception and basic assumption that the leadership style that is most effective is the one that takes into account a high degree of task orientation and a high degree of person orientation (Yukl, 1994).

2.2.1.3 Situation-Oriented Approaches

The situation-oriented approaches establish connections of leadership behaviour in and to various situation-related contexts. These include, for example, the *life-cycle theory* and its maturity model according to Hersey and Blanchard (1969), in which leadership styles are differentiated depending on the task orientation or competence and expertise of the leader as well as the quality of the relationship between leader and led (see Fig. 2.2).

The division into high and low degrees of relationship and task orientation results in four quadrants in the coordinate system. Starting from the bottom right, different situational leadership styles can be described in a counterclockwise direction regarding the expertise of the employee and the leader-follower relationship. *Firstly*, if the maturity level of the person being led is not particularly high, i.e. the person has not yet acquired many competences in the relevant area and the relationship orientation is low, e.g. because there has not yet been sufficient joint work experience, then the task should be discussed explicitly and in detail ("telling" or "instruction"; authoritarian leadership style). *Secondly*, the quadrant at the top right shows that in a situation where employees do not yet have a comprehensive level of knowledge in the relevant area of work, a high level of relationship orientation on the part of the supervisor is required, i.e. shared experiential knowledge. In that situation, the focus is on "selling" (integrated leadership style). In other words, the employees should be convinced of the importance of the task, and it must be explained why this

2.2 Typology of Leadership Approaches

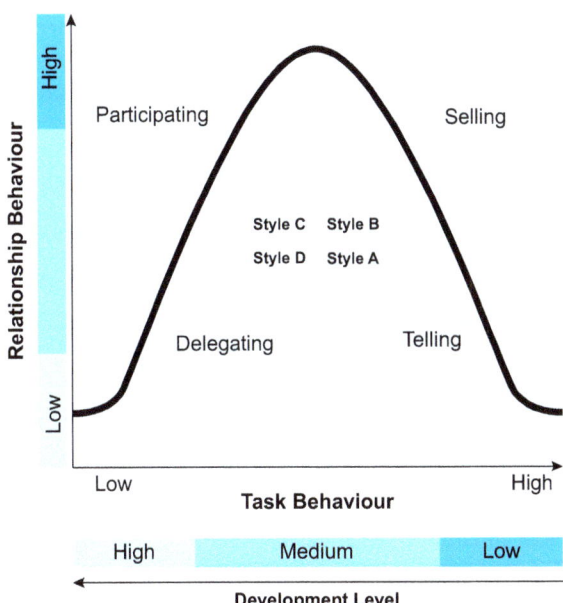

Fig. 2.2 Situational leadership by Hersey and Blanchard (1969), as cited in Lippold, 2019, p. 22 (Adapted and translated by permission from Springer Nature: *Klassische Führungsansätze und -theorien*. In: *Führungskultur im Wandel* by Dirk Lippold. © 2019 Springer Fachmedien Wiesbaden GmbH, a part of Springer Nature; author's translation)

task is of high significance for the organisation. *Thirdly*, in the top left quadrant, a participative leadership style is illustrated ("participating"). In this case, the task orientation is low, i.e. the person in question already has the necessary competence in the task area and the leader has a long-term relationship with the person being led. *Finally*, the fourth quadrant on the bottom left describes the leadership style of "delegating". Here, the task orientation is low, i.e. the person has an advanced level of competence or experience in the task area and the relationship orientation is low. For task clarification and implementation, it is not absolutely necessary for the employee to have everything explained in detail, but rather the leader assumes that the employee can implement the task independently and autonomously without much guidance or consultation with their superior. Consequently, the task can simply be delegated. This model has been criticised, among other things, because various empirical studies have found no evidence supporting it. Thus, it retains the character of a theory, with the maturity level of employees considered as the only person-oriented variable in the complex model (Northouse, 2016, p. 100). Nevertheless, it has proven to be a very practicable model that offers a degree of orientation and flexibility for everyday leadership. Sometimes a good theory can also be very helpful for good practice.

Based on the life-cycle model, the *contingency theory* of leadership effectiveness (contingency model) assumes that the leader's natural leadership style should be used to produce the best leadership performance. Instead, Fiedler's (1965, 1967) contingency model of leadership effectiveness assumes that a leader must first be "placed in a situation in which he or she can achieve the best leadership performance according to his or her natural leadership style" (von Au, 2016, p. 11, transl.

MA). In the framework of Fiedler's *least preferred coworker (LPC) scale*, three variables or factors are linked: "'relationship between leader and those being led', 'task structure' and 'positional power' [...] which together determine the 'favourability' of the situation for leadership success" (von Au, 2016, p. 12, transl. MA). Contingency theory has been criticised for failing to provide recommendations on how to change leaders (or their leadership styles) or conditions that do not match (Lippold, 2019, p. 17). Additionally, the theory does not attempt to explain why specific leadership styles are successful or not in particular contexts.

Vroom and Yetton (1973) and later Vroom and Jago (2007) have argued within their normative decision-making model that the most appropriate leadership style always depends on the situation. This model prefers the choice of a particular leadership style for group decision-making and identifies five different leadership styles (from autocratic to consultative to group-based decision-making) depending on the situation and the level of participation. In this context, six criteria are used to structure situations in the leadership interaction between managers and employees: quality requirement, degree of information, problem structure, acceptance by employees, goal congruence and degree of conflict (von Au, 2016, p. 12). As already noted, this is a decision model and "[j]ust according to the assessment of these criteria, different situationally appropriate leadership styles result in a decision tree, ranging from an authoritarian decision by the manager to a consultative involvement of the employees in the decision-making process to group decision-making in the team" (von Au, 2016, p. 12).

In the context of situational leadership in the early 1970s, for example, Evans' (1970) and House's (1971) *path-goal theories* expanded the understanding of leadership behaviour and task orientation to include as third dimension the follower motivation, which has a significant influence on leadership interaction. In each case, the leadership behaviour that best suits the employees and the work environment is identified, depending on the extent to which following a certain behaviour (path) leads to a certain result (goal). The aim is to increase motivation, empowerment and satisfaction of employees so that they can contribute productively to the organisation and remove potential obstacles. Despite these positive features, the validity of the path-goal theory remains provisional, as the research findings to date do not provide a complete and consistent picture of the basic assumptions; conclusions of the path-goal theory have only been partially supported by empirical studies (Schriesheim et al., 2006; Northouse, 2016, p. 123).

Reddin (1967) developed the so-called *3-D management model*, which can also be categorised as a situational leadership approach. The model is based on task orientation and relationship orientation (similar to the life-cycle model) as well as on the four main leadership styles identified in the Ohio studies: the procedural, relational, integrative and task-oriented leadership styles. Reddin (1967) assumes that all latter leadership styles can be efficient and successful in different situations. According to Reddin's 3-D model, leaders must employ all four leadership styles depending on the scenario. This great degree of adaptability demanded of leaders requires specific training (Lippold, 2019, p. 21).

2.2 Typology of Leadership Approaches

In general, situational leadership approaches are criticised for remaining mostly on a theoretical level and for being difficult to measure and operationalise. In contrast to many other leadership theories, the situational approaches lack comparable research findings to justify and support the theoretical foundations on which they are ultimately based. Also, it is often not clearly elaborated how leaders can (further) develop in different development phases or how their engagement changes over time (Northouse, 2016, pp. 112–113).

2.2.2 New Leadership Approaches

The *new leadership approaches* can be understood as a reaction to sociocultural, political and economic changes in organisational environment that took place over the course of the twentieth century and the associated transformation of values from "values of duty and acceptance to values of self-development and autonomy" (von Au, 2016, p. 13, transl. MA). In contrast to the classical approaches, complex and integrative leadership theories are in the foreground, which can be characterised in particular by the following basic dimensions according to the InLeaVe® new leadership model (von Au, 2016, pp. 13–18): (1) interaction, (2) system, (3) participation and (4) meaning. The levels presented below are based on Au's (2016) overview (cf. also Fig. 2.3).

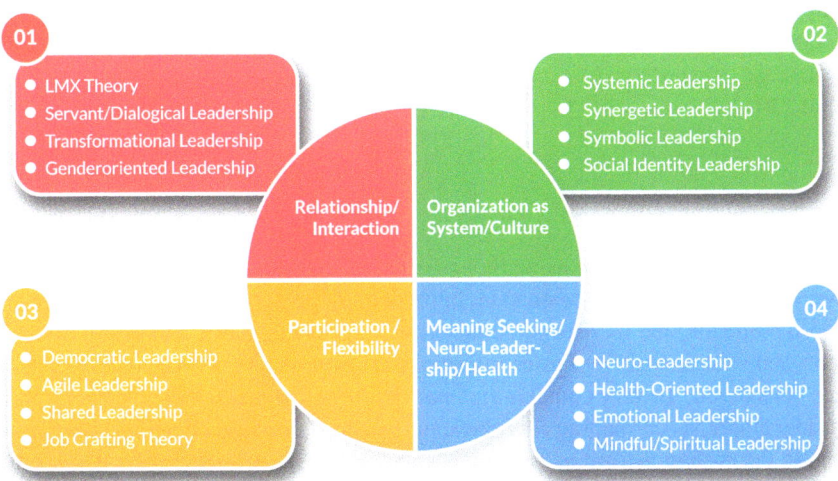

Fig. 2.3 New leadership approaches. (Reprinted from Arnold, 2022, licenced under CC BY 4.0, extended and adapted from von Au, 2016, p. 6; author's translation)

2.2.2.1 Interaction and Relationship Level

The new leadership approaches focus on the qualities of the leadership interaction itself. Leadership is seen as an all-round transformative process in which implicit values and beliefs such as the granting of individual development opportunities and the achievement of performance gains become important. In this context, the *leader-member exchange theory (LMX)* (Graen & Uhl-Bien, 1995) assumes different forms of a reciprocal relationship between leader and follower based on trust and respect. In addition, the approaches of servant leadership, emotional leadership and dialogical leadership can also be assigned to this dimension. In the *servant leadership* approach according to Greenleaf (1977), the servant leader is expected to inspire and involve their followers in making things happen, rather than motivating them through formal coercive and over-subordinate relationships. Closely related to this is Goleman et al.'s (2002, p. 14) *emotional leadership* theory, according to which leaders must be able to arouse "emotions people feel while they work" by creating "resonance". *Dialogical leadership* (Dietz & Kracht, 2011) finally works on the idea of how, if possible, a multitude of stakeholders in an organisation can be brought into an ongoing dialogue and, thus, enable productive cooperation. Within the transformational leadership approach, first described by Burns (1978) towards the end of the 1970s, leaders and led are "transformed" by the meaning-making and empowerment-promoting aspects of tasks and job opportunities, inspirational motivation, intellectual stimulation, individual promotion and idealised influence (Bass & Avolio, 1994). In this process, the leader facilitates sense-making, formulation and communication of vision and mobilisation of those being led. This is also emphasised in more recent gender-oriented approaches (cf. in more detail Hernandez Bark et al., 2017). According to the difference theory, for example, people in organisations have differently connoted personality traits and set expectations for leadership, and according to the androgyny theory (Bem, 1974), leaders are able to "combine masculine connoted and feminine connoted personality traits in their behaviour" regardless of gender, age, origin, etc. (von Au, 2016, p. 15; Kark et al., 2012).

2.2.2.2 System Level

Leadership action is fundamentally embedded in a systemic context and cannot be controlled directly from the outside. In particular, the dynamics between the inside and the outside, the increasing complexity, multi-layeredness, ambiguity of problems and situations as well as organisations as learning and self-regulating systems are considered. In this context, *systemic leadership* means that managers place greater emphasis on shaping communication contexts and the organisational culture within the system as well as dependency and exchange relationships with all other stakeholders (e.g. employees, clients, suppliers) (for an overview, see Arnold, 2017; Schmid, 2016): "Systemically acting managers set development processes in motion and improve structures and relationships in organisations due to their personality and attitude" (von Au, 2016, p. 15). Graf et al. (2017) use the *synergetic leadership* approach, which assumes that leadership depends on the promotion and control of various tasks within the organisation: difference management (differentiation from surrounding systems), resource management (allocation of resources in the team), structure management (clear distribution of roles and responsibilities), process management (definition of time sequence), reflection management (improvement through monitoring and feedback) and development management (outsourcing and request for support). In addition, *symbolic leadership* focuses on the meaningful actions of the leader (e.g. written or verbal communication) (von Rosenstiel, 2014). Here, the symbols, rituals and traditions relevant for shaping the organisational culture as well as the basic assumptions are in the foreground. In contrast, the *social identity leadership model* (cf. Hogg & van Knippenberg, 2003) considers the always situation- and context-specific connection between personality and the "prototypical fit with the group", which leaders constantly have to work on (Hernandez Bark et al., 2017, p. 98, transl. MA).

2.2.2.3 Participation and Flexibilisation

In contrast to classical leadership approaches, which more often invoke charismatic and authoritarian leaders, newer approaches such as agile leadership, shared leadership and job crafting leadership emphasise participation and agility in collaboration: *Agile leadership* focuses on responding quickly to changing conditions, customer demands and product changes, with an emphasis on cross-functional collaboration, short-term and interactive performance reviews, continuous reflection and a living-learning culture (e.g. Häusling & Rutz, 2017). In this context, Raelin (2003) speaks of so-called leaderful practice, a form of collective leadership that differs from "conventional" leadership:

> Conventional leadership is based on a hierarchical and controlling management model. Leaderful Practice, on the other hand, represents a consistent continuation of the organic-systemic leadership approach. Strength comes from community, appreciation, and support, which allows major challenges to be met quickly and efficiently. (von Au, 2016, p. 16, transl. MA)

In *shared leadership* (e.g. Werther, 2013, p. 13), tasks and associated responsibilities are assigned to several formal or informal leaders jointly or on a rotating basis, with all those involved in the leadership process striving to achieve common goals. Leaders must also have self-leadership skills within the framework of team-oriented leadership. This is also closely related to *job crafting leadership*, according to which leaders perform the role of proactive and change-initiating change managers, which has an impact on job design and satisfaction and promotes employees in terms of their interests and strengths. Müller (2017) distinguishes three strategies of job crafting in this context: changing the scope of tasks, working relationships and the perception of the work itself.

2.2.2.4 Meaning Level

Increasingly, new trends such as self-development, mindfulness in times of resilience and health promotion, but also emotional intelligence and spiritual leadership as well as the inclusion of neuroscientific findings, are moving to the centre of the discussion of leadership. *Neuroleadership* (Ghadiri et al., 2013) in the sense of "brain-friendly" leadership postulates:

> [t]hat change is a pain in the form of physiological effort through the reorganisation of networks in the brain ('change is pain'). In this context, neurostress, i.e. biochemical changes caused by permanent stress and the resulting stress-related illnesses as well as illnesses with strong psychological symptoms, such as depression, burnout, anxiety disorders and addictions, but which are largely physical, i.e. metabolic, is of particular importance. (von Au, 2016, p. 17, transl. MA)

Consequently, the "psychological well-being" of people in organisations should be promoted, which has a considerable influence on their performance and the quality of results. In this context, psychological well-being is differentiated by Grawe (2004) on four levels: striving for consistency, striving for need satisfaction, motivational (approach and avoidance) schemas and the behavioural level. In this context, the promotion and development of mindfulness and attentiveness in leadership also have a special role to play in contributing to "healthy" leadership in the workplace and for all who are led through reflective and mindful self-leadership (von Au, 2016).

The new leadership approaches – as has been shown – go beyond the classical approaches and recognise more strongly that leadership is a multidimensional phenomenon which depends on many more competences, factors and variables than those which define the leader (e.g. relationship/interaction, system, participation, meaning). We will leave it at this brief overview, as selected newer leadership approaches will be discussed in detail in Chap. 4.

2.2.2.5 Overview of Recent Leadership Approaches

Against the background of the levels and dimensions presented above, various other recent leadership approaches can be summarised as follows (cf. Table 2.3).

2.2 Typology of Leadership Approaches

Table 2.3 Overview on new leadership theories

Approaches	Authors	Main statements	Critical evaluation
Super leadership theory	Manz and Sims (1987, 1989)	*Idea:* Belongs to the transformational leadership approach; decentralised, geographically dispersed and temporally staggered work environment, whereby leaders can exert little influence on employee behaviour. *Basic assumptions:* Motivation of employees to self-organise and self-lead; supervisors as process facilitators. *Implementation:* Introduction of self-management principles based on the company's values and strategies to empower employees to perform tasks and make decisions independently.	Leadership success is largely decoupled from the leader. Super leadership approach not useful in all areas and sectors (Weibler, 2016, p. 390).
Shared leadership	Craig L. Pearce and Sims (2001, 2002); Pearce and Conger (2002)	*Idea:* In contrast to classic leadership hierarchies, which are usually dominated by "sole decision-makers", here the functional pyramid is put aside. *Basic assumptions:* Leaders and those being led interact as "equals" in the leadership process, with leaders responsible for supporting, motivating and mobilising those being led. *Implementation* requires perseverance and trust in the implementation of the approach.	Promotion of trust among team members, higher group performance and satisfaction necessary. "Lack of orientation" or "abuse of power" by team members, if applicable "According to research results, a high proportion of women, combined with an overall low average age, crystallised as a favourable factor for introduction. In addition, a high ethnic diversity and a high level of mutual trust within the group also counted" (Lippold, 2019, p. 32, transl. MA) Fears, apprehensions in dealing with non-directive leadership behaviour.

(continued)

Table 2.3 (continued)

Approaches	Authors	Main statements	Critical evaluation
Distributed leadership	Bolden (2011); Benson and Blackman (2011)	*Idea:* Leadership goes beyond the group and can be distributed in terms of situational flexibility, strategic, geographical, functional and cultural aspects. *Basic assumptions:* "In principle, shared and distributed leadership approaches always have a particular relevance when it comes to sharing and distributing leadership tasks, sharing leadership responsibilities, sharing and distributing power resources, and exercising influence jointly and collectively" (Lippold, 2019, p. 32, transl. MA). *Implementation:* Implies tacit agreement and acceptance by all other leaders in the organisation.	High flexibility and fluidity in leadership distribution. Success requires direct coordination between leaders: "The distribution of leadership, to changing other persons, is thus here a situationally coordinated exceptional case that is ended as soon as the overload or danger situation is over" (Endres & Weibler, 2019, p. 9, transl. MA).

(continued)

2.2 Typology of Leadership Approaches

Table 2.3 (continued)

Approaches	Authors	Main statements	Critical evaluation
Agile leadership	e.g. Highsmith (2009)	*Idea:* This is a specific form of shared leadership, whereby it is oriented towards the competences of the employees, and leadership is understood as being guided by values and principles. *Basic assumptions:* The term agility encompasses various levels: Agile values and principles (see agile manifest always, agile methods (e.g. scrum, Kanban, design thinking) as well as agile practices, techniques and tools. It requires "replacing rigid planning with lean, manageable planning, and implementation cycles with concrete results and working interdisciplinarily in short iterations to be able to act and react quickly" (von Au, 2016, p. 28, transl. MA). In agile organisations, "employees form into squads (interdisciplinary product teams), tribes (grouping of squads with a common business mission) and chapters (focal points of knowledge and experience across squads) to form constantly new teams. The leadership organisation comprises Product Owners (process owners within a Squad), Tribe Leads (management leaders within a Tribe) and Chapter Leads (hierarchical function with holistic personnel responsibility within a Chapter). In addition, agile coaches offer individual coaching of individuals or facilitation of teams" (Jochmann, 2019 cited in Lippold, 2019, p. 34, transl. MA). *Implementation:* Employees implement their tasks in a self-determined way and are actively involved in decisions.	Agile methods have proven themselves in practice, especially in project work. Empirical studies confirm that agile methods are used in many companies (Komus & Kuberg, 2017). Necessary preconditions for success are organisational strategy, structure and culture with an agile focus, implementation of agile methods, transfer of responsibility to the team and flexible personnel development methods.

(continued)

Table 2.3 (continued)

Approaches	Authors	Main statements	Critical evaluation
Virtual leadership (leadership with new media)	Caulat (2006, 2012); DeRosa and Lepsinger (2010); Wald (2014)	*Idea:* The focus is on leadership of employees with the help of modern information and communication technologies or social media to bridge spatial and temporal distances. *Basic assumptions:* It deals with changed leadership relationships and focuses on relationship building and maintenance: "The lack of personal connection and information on the social context makes is difficult to build social relationships and trust. This can cause passivity and a reluctance to perform on the part of employees. On the other hand, dealing with this distance, i.e., successful communication with modern media, as well as building and maintaining trust, become indispensable under virtual conditions" (Lippold, 2019, p. 36, transl. MA). *Implementation:* Leadership is distributed across different instances against the background of virtual working relationships, so that the self-direction capability of the team and other employees is enabled, such as through shared, transactional, transformational and participative leadership styles.	Implementation is associated with various contradictions: Overcoming distances; the use of new ways of communication; the distribution of leadership tasks is on the one hand causes and on the other hand a consequence. There is currently a lack of further empirical studies to substantiate effects. The practice of virtual leadership depends very much on the skills and abilities of the leaders, such as communication and consultation skills, media skills, promotion of trust building, participatory expectation and needs management as well as practical skills for managing virtual projects (Wald, 2014, p. 375).

(continued)

2.2 Typology of Leadership Approaches

Table 2.3 (continued)

Approaches	Authors	Main statements	Critical evaluation
Digital leadership	e.g. Jameson (2013)	*Idea*: Digital leadership competence is a bundle of different competences that include "personal competences (e.g., loyalty, credibility, personal responsibility) activity and action competences (e.g., drive, decision-making, initiative), technical and methodological competences (e.g., expertise, planning behaviour, market knowledge), and social-communicative competences (e.g., communication, integration, teamwork skills)" (Erpenbeck & Heyse, 1999 as cited in Lippold, 2019, p. 38, transl. MA). *Basic assumptions*: Leadership competence is to be included as a cross-cutting competence (e.g. communication skills, decision-making skills, teamwork skills) and is supplemented by media competence and intercultural competence. *Implementation*: Various promoters participate in the following phases: (1) *pre-phase*, initiation and identification of the need for change; (2) *digital strategy development* (i.e. conceptualisation and goal setting); (3) *transformation process* (i.e. mobilisation of staff, implementation through project and quality management, personal development, implementation of results); and (4) *monitoring and optimisation* (Arnold, 2021).	Benefits of digital leadership are increased employee responsibility as well as participation and increased communication in the workplace through different communication channels. Equally, some disadvantages are obvious: Loss of interpersonal communication opportunities, dependency and effective implementation on the technology used, increasing costs, resistance from employees in the change process, data security, challenges for work-life balance.

Lippold, 2019, pp. 30–40 (Reprinted and translated by permission from Springer Nature: *Klassische Führungsansätze und -theorien. In: Führungskultur im Wandel* by Dirk Lippold. © 2019 Springer Fachmedien Wiesbaden GmbH, a part of Springer Nature); Endres & Weibler, 2019; Erpenbeck & Heyse, 1999; Weibler, 2016; von Au, 2016; Wald, 2014; author's translation

References

Algahtani, A. (2014). Are leadership and management different? A review. *Journal of Management Policies and Practices, 2*(3), 71–82. https://doi.org/10.15640/jmpp.v2n3a4

Arnold, M. (2017). Diakonische Praxis und ihre Gestaltung in Organisationen. In M. Arnold, D. Bonchino-Demmler, R. Evers, M. Hussmann, & U. Liedke (Hrsg.), *Perspektiven diakonischer Profilentwicklung: Ein Arbeitsbuch am Beispiel von Einrichtungen der Diakonie in Sachsen* (pp. 28-48). Leipzig: EVA.

Arnold, M. (2021). Leading Digital Change and the Management of Hybridity in Social Work Organizations. In Özsungur, F. (Ed.), *Handbook of Research on Policies, Protocols, and Practices for Social Work in the Digital World* (pp. 55–73). IGI Global. https://doi.org/10.4018/978-1-7998-7772-1.ch004

Arnold, M. (2022). *New leadership approaches* (Version1). [figshare]. https://doi.org/10.6084/m9.figshare.20079863.v1.

Arnold, M., Bonchino-Demmler, D., & Hußmann, M. (2017). Einblicke: Die empirische Untersuchung »Perspektiven Diakonischer Profilentwicklung am Beispiel von Einrichtungen der Diakonie in Sachsen«. In M. Arnold, D. Bonchino-Demmler, R. Evers, M. Hußmann, & U. Liedke, (Eds), *Perspektiven diakonischer Profilbildung: Ein Arbeitsbuch am Beispiel von Einrichtungen der Diakonie in Sachsen* (pp. 253–268). EVA.

Barge, J. K. (1994). *Leadership: Communication skills for organizations and groups*. St Martin's Press.

Bass, B. M. (1985). *Leadership and performance beyond expectations*. Free Press.

Bass, B. M. (1990a). *Bass and Stogdill's handbook of leadership: Theory, research, and managerial applications*. Free Press.

Bass, B. M. (1990b). From transactional to transformational leadership: Learning to share the vision. *Organizational Dynamics, 18*, 19–31.

Bass, B. M., & Avolio, B. J. (Eds.). (1994). *Improving organizational effectiveness through transformational leadership*. SAGE.

Bass, B. M., & Bass, R. (2009). *The Bass handbook of leadership: Theory, research, and managerial applications*. Free Press.

Bem, S. L. (1974). The measurement of psychological androgyny. *Journal of Consulting and Clinical Psychology, 42*, 155–162.

Bennis, W. G. (1989). Managing the dream: Leadership in the 21st century. *Journal of Organizational Change Management, 2*(1), 6–10.

Bennis, W. (1998). Managers do things right. Leaders do the right thing. In C. Kennedy (Ed.), *Management Gurus: 40 Vordenker und ihre Ideen* (pp. 47–52). Gabler Verlag. https://doi.org/10.1007/978-3-322-82771-5_7

Bennis, W. G., & Goldsmith, J. (1997). *Learning to Lead: A workbook on becoming a leader*. Addison-Wesley.

Bennis, W. G., Spreitzer, G. M., & Cummings, T. G. (2001). *The future of leadership: Today's top leadership thinkers speak to tomorrow's leaders*. Jossey-Bass.

Benson, A. M., & Blackman, D. (2011). To distribute leadership or not? A lesson from the islands. *Tourism Management, 32*(5), 1141–1149. https://doi.org/10.1016/j.tourman.2010.10.002

Birch, P. (1999). *Instant leadership*. Kogan Page.

Blake, R. R., & Mouton, J. S. (1964). *The new managerial grid: Key orientations for achieving production through people*. Gulf Publishing Company.

Bolden, R. (2011). Distributed leadership in organizations: A review of theory and research. *International Journal of Management Reviews, 13*, 251–269.

Bowers, D. G., & Seashore, S. E. (1966). Predicting organizational effectiveness with a four-factor theory of leadership. *Administrative Science Quarterly, 11*(2), 238–263.

Brose, P., & Hentzel, J. (1990). *Personalführungslehre: Grundlagen, Führungsstile, Funktion und Theorien der Führung*. Schäffer-Poeschel.

Bryman, A. (1992). *Charisma and leadership in organizations*. SAGE.

References

Bryman, A., Collinson, D., Grint, K., Jackson, G., & Uhl-Bien, M. (Eds.). (2011). *The SAGE handbook of leadership*. SAGE.
Buchanan, D. A., & Huczynski, A. A. (2019). *Organizational behaviour*. Pearson UK.
Burns, J. M. (1978). *Leadership*. Harper & Row.
Caulat, G. (2006). Virtual leadership. *The Ashridge Journal, 3*, 6–11.
Caulat, G. (2012). *Virtual leadership: Learning to Lead differently*. Libri.
Certo, S. C. (1997). *Modern Management*. Prentice Hall.
Chapman, E. N. (1989). *Leadership*. Prentice Hall.
Day, D. V., & Antonakis, J. (Eds.). (2012). *The nature of leadership* (2nd ed.). SAGE.
DeRosa, D., & Lepsinger, R. (2010). *Virtual team success*. Jossey-Bass.
Dietz, K.-M., & Kracht, K. (2011). *Dialogische Führung: Grundlagen, Praxis, Fallbeispiel: dm-Drogeriemarkt* (3rd ed.). Frankfurt a. M.
Drucker, P. (2013). *Managing for the future*. Taylor and Francis.
Eck, C. D. (2007). Führung-Leadership: Thesen und Hypothesen zu einem Irrlicht der Praxis und Theorie der Organisationsgestaltung. In R. Ballreich, M. W. Fröse, & H. Piper (Eds.), *Organisationsentwicklung und Konfliktmanagement: Innovative Konzepte und Methoden* (pp. 9–38). Haupt.
Endres, S., & Weibler, J. (2019). *Plural Leadership: Eine zukunftsweisende Alternative zur One-Man-Show*. Springer. https://doi.org/10.1007/978-3-658-27116-9
Erpenbeck, J., & Heyse, V. (1999). *Die Kompetenzbiographie* (Studien zur beruflichen Weiterbildung im Transformationsprozess, Band 10). Waxmann.
Evans, M. G. (1970). The effects of supervisory behavior on the path-goal relationship. *Organizational Behavior and Human Performance, 5*, 277–298.
Fairhurst, G. T. (2011). Discursive approaches to leadership. In A. Bryman, D. Collinson, K. Grint, B. Jackson, & M. Uhl-Bien (Eds.), *The Sage handbook of leadership* (pp. 495–507). Sage.
Fiedler, F. E. (1965). Engineer the job to fit the manager. *Harvard Business Review, 43*(5), 115–122.
Fiedler, F. E. (1967). *A theory of leadership effectiveness*. McGraw Hill.
Fröse, M. (2015). *Transformationen in ›sozialen‹ Organisationen: Verborgene Komplexitäten. Ein Entwurf*. Würzburg: Ergon.
Fröse, M. W., Naake, B., & Arnold, M. (2019). Quo Vadis - leadership und organisation. In M. W. Fröse, B. Naake, & M. Arnold (Eds.), *Führung und Organisation: Neue Entwicklungen im Management der Sozial- und Gesundheitswirtschaft* (pp. 1–30). Springer. https://doi.org/10.1007/978-3-658-24193-3_1
Gardner, H. (2011). *Leading minds - an anatomy of leadership*. Basic Books.
Ghadiri, A., Habermacher, A., & Peters, T. (2013). *Neuroleadership: A journey through the brain for business leaders*. Springer. https://doi.org/10.1007/978-3-642-30165-0
Goethals, G. R., Sorenson, G. J., & Burns, J. M. G. (2004). *Encyclopedia of leadership* (Vol. 4). SAGE.
Goldberg, L. R. (1990). An alternative "description of personality": The big-five factor structure. *Journal of Personality and Social Psychology, 59*, 1216–1229.
Goleman, D., Boyatzis, R., & McKee, A. (2002). *Primal leadership: Realizing the power of emotional intelligence*. Harvard Business School Press.
Graen, G. B., & Uhl-Bien, M. (1995). Relationship-based approach to leadership: Development of Leader-Member Exchange (LMX) theory of leadership over 25 years: Applying a multi-level multi-domain perspective. *Leadership Quarterly, 25*, 219–247.
Graf, N., Könnecke, C., & Witte, E. (2017). Synergetische Führung – Systemsteuerung als Führungsaufgabe. In C. von Au (Hrsg.), *Struktur und Kultur einer Leadership-Organisation: Holistik, Wertschätzung, Vertrauen, Agilität und Lernen* (pp. 123–140). Springer. https://doi.org/10.1007/978-3-658-12554-7_7.
Grawe, K. (2004). *Neuropsychotherapie*. Hogrefe Verlag.
Greenleaf, R. K. (1977). *Servant leadership: A journey into the nature of legitimate power and greatness*. Paulist Press.

Halpin, A. W., & Winer, B. J. (1957). A factorial study of the leader behavior descriptions. In R. M. Stogdill & A. E. Coons (Eds.), *Leader behavior: Its description and measurement*. Ohio State University, Bureau of Business Research, No. 88.

Häusling, A., & Rutz, B. (2017). Agile Führungsstruktur und -kultur zur Förderung der Selbstorganisation - Ausgestaltung und Herausforderungen. In C. von Au (Ed.), *Struktur und Kultur einer Leadership-Organisation: Holistik, Wertschätzung, Vertrauen, Agilität und Lernen* (pp. 105–122). Springer. https://doi.org/10.1007/978-3-658-12554-7_6

Hemphill, J. K., & Coons, A. E. (1957). Development of the leader behavior description questionnaire. In R. M. Stogdill & A. E. Coons (Eds.), *Leader behavior: Its description and measurement*. Ohio State University, Bureau of Business Research, No. 88.

Hendry, J. (2013). *Management: A very short introduction*. Oxford University Press.

Hernandez Bark, A. S., von Quaquebeke, N., & von Dick, R. (2017). Wird Führung weiblicher? Warum Krisen nach anderer Führung verlangen. In C. von Au (Ed.), *Struktur und Kultur einer Leadership-Organisation: Holistik, Wertschätzung, Vertrauen, Agilität und Lernen* (pp. 89–104). Springer. https://doi.org/10.1007/978-3-658-12554-7_5

Hersey, P., & Blanchard, K. H. (1969). Life cycle theory of leadership. *Training and Development Journal, 23*(2), 26–34.

Hickman, G. R. (Ed.). (2009). *Leading organizations: Perspectives for a new era* (2nd ed.). SAGE.

Highsmith, J. A. (2009). *Agile Project Management: Creating innovative products* (1st ed.). Pearson Education.

Hinterhuber, H. H. (2009). Führen heißt die Herzen der Mitarbeiterinnen und Mitarbeiter gewinnen. In J. Eurich & A. Brink (Eds.), *Leadership in sozialen Organisationen* (pp. 21–29). VS.

Hogg, M. A., & van Knippenberg, D. (2003). Social identity and leadership processes in groups. In M. P. Zanna (Ed.), *Advances in experimental social psychology* (Vol. 35, pp. 1–52). Academic.

House, R. J. (1971). A path-goal theory of leader effectiveness. *Administrative Science Quarterly, 16*, 321–328.

House, R. J. (1977). A theory of charismatic leadership. In J. G. Hunt & L. L. Larson (Eds.), *Leadership: The cutting edge* (pp. 189–207). Southern Illinois University Press.

Jameson, J. (2013). Special issue on e-leadership: Editorial. *British Journal of Educational Technology, 44*(6), 883–888. https://doi.org/10.1111/bjet.12106

Jochmann, W. (2019). *Top Trends in HR und People Management 2019*. https://www.linkedin.com/pulse/toptrends-hr-und-people-management-2019-dr-walter-jochmann/

John, O. P., Naumann, L. P., & Soto, C. J. (2008). Paradigm shift to the integrative big five trait taxonomy: History, measurement, and conceptual issues. In O. P. John, R. W. Robins, & L. A. Pervin (Eds.), *Handbook of personality: Theory and research* (pp. 114–158). The Guilford Press.

Judge, T. A., Bono, J. E., Ilies, R., & Gerhardt, M. W. (2002). Personality and leadership: A qualitative and quantitative review. *Journal of Applied Psychology, 4*(87), 765–780.

Kark, R., Waismel-Manor, R., & Shamir, B. (2012). Does valuing androgyny and femininity lead to a female advantage? The relationship between gender-role, transformational leadership and identification. *The Leadership Quarterly, 23*, 620–640.

Katz, R. L. (1955). Skills of an effective administrator. *Harvard Business Review, 33*(1), 33–42.

Komus, A., & Kuberg, M. (2017). *Status Quo Agile: Studie zu Verbreitung und Nutzen agiler Methoden: Eine empirische Untersuchung*. GPM Deutsche Gesellschaft für Projektmanagement e. V.

Kotter, J. P. (1990a). What leaders really do. *Harvard Business Review, 79*(11), 85–97.

Kotter, J. P. (1990b). *A force for change: How leadership differs from management*. Free Press.

Kotterman, J. (2006). Leadership vs management: What's the difference? *Journal for Quality & Participation, 29*(2), 13–17.

Lewin, K., Lippitt, R., & White, R. K. (1939). Patterns of aggressive behavior in experimentally created social climates. *Journal of Science Psychology, 10*, 271–299.

Lippold, D. (2019). *Führungskultur im Wandel: Klassische und moderne Führungsansätze im Zeitalter der Digitalisierung*. Springer Gabler. https://doi.org/10.1007/978-3-658-25855-9

References

Lunenburg, F. C. (2011). Leadership versus management: A key distinction—At least in theory. *International Journal of Management, Business, and Administration, 14*(1), 1–4.

Manz, C. C., & Sims, H. P. (1987). Leading workers to lead themselves: The external leadership of self-managed working teams. *Administrative Science Quarterly, 32*, 106–128.

Manz, C. C., & Sims, H. P. (1989). *Superleadership: Leading others to lead themselves*. Prentice-Hall.

Marston, W. M. (1928). *Emotions of normal people*. K. Paul, Trench, Trubner & Ltd.

McCrae, R. R., & Costa, P. T. (1987). Validation of the five-factor model of personality across instruments and observers. *Journal of Personality and Social Psychology, 52*, 81–90.

Moore, B. V. (1927). The may conference on leadership. *The Personnel Journal, 6*, 124–128.

Morgan, G. (1986). *Images of organization*. Sage.

Müller, E. B. (2017). Job crafting leadership. In C. von Au (Ed.), *Struktur und Kultur einer Leadership-Organisation: Holistik, Wertschätzung, Vertrauen, Agilität und Lernen* (pp. 141–156). Springer. https://doi.org/10.1007/978-3-658-12554-7_8

Mumford, M. D. (2006). *Pathways to outstanding leadership: A comparative analysis of charismatic, ideological, and pragmatic leaders*. Lawrence Erlbaum.

Mumford, M. D., Zaccaro, S. J., Harding, F. D., Jacobs, T. O., & Fleishman, E. A. (2000). Leadership skills for a changing world: Solving complex social problems. *Leadership Quarterly, 11*(1), 11–35.

Neuberger, O. (2002). *Führen und führen lassen: Ansätze, Ergebnisse und Kritik der Führungsforschung* (6th ed.). Utb.

Northouse, P. G. (2016). *Leadership: Theory and practice* (7th ed.). Sage.

Oxford English Dictionary. (2022). *Manage*. https://www.oxfordlearnersdictionaries.com/definition/english/manage

Pearce, C. L., & Conger, J. A. (2002). *Shared leadership: Reframing the hows and whys of leadership*. SAGE. https://doi.org/10.4135/9781452229539

Pearce, C. L., & Sims, H. P. (2001). Shared leadership: Toward a multi-level theory of leadership. *Advances in Interdisciplinary Studies of Work Teams, 7*, 115–139. https://doi.org/10.1016/S1572-0977(00)07008-4

Pearce, C. L., & Sims, H. P. (2002). Vertical versus shared leadership as predictors of the effectiveness of change management teams: An examination of aversive, directive, transactional, transformational, and empowering leader behaviors. *Group Dynamics, 6*, 172–197. https://doi.org/10.1037//1089-2699.6.2.172

Raelin, J. A. (2003). *Creating leaderful organizations*. Berrett-Koehler.

Reddin, W. J. (1967). The 3-D management style theory. *Training and Development Journal, 21*(4), 8–17.

Rigotti, F. (1994). *Die Macht und die Metaphern: Über die sprachlichen Bilder der Politik*. Frankfurt a. M.: Campus.

Rost, J. C. (1991). *Leadership for the twenty-first century*. Praeger.

Schein, E. (1992). *Organisational culture and leadership* (5th ed.). Wiley.

Schmid, B. (2016). Führen aus systemischer Sicht. In C. von Au (Ed.), *Wirksame und nachhaltige Führungsansätze: System, Beziehung, Haltung und Individualität* (pp. 135–152). Springer. https://doi.org/10.1007/978-3-658-11956-0

Schriesheim, C. A., Castro, S. L., Zhou, X., & DeChurch, L. A. (2006). An investigation of path-goal and transformational leadership theory predictions at the individual level of analysis. *Leadership Quarterly, 17*, 21–38.

Steinle, C. (1978). *Führung. Grundlagen, Prozesse und Modelle der Führung in der Unternehmung*. C.E. Poeschel.

Stock-Homburg, R. (2013). *Personal management: Theorien - Konzepte – Instrumente* (3rd ed.). Springer Gabler.

Stogdill, R. M. (1948). Personal factors associated with leadership: A survey of the literature. *Journal of Psychology, 25*, 35–71.

Stogdill, R. M. (1974). *Handbook of leadership: A survey of theory and research*. Free Press.

Tannenbaum, R., & Schmidt, W. H. (1973). How to choose a leadership pattern. *Harvard Business Review, 51*(3), 162–180.

Tourish, D., & Jackson, B. (2008). Guest editorial: Communication and leadership: An open invitation to engage. *Leadership, 4*(3), 219–225.

Uhl-Bien, M., Maslyn, J., & Ospina, S. (2012). The nature of relational leadership: A multitheoretical lens on leadership relationships and processes. In D. V. Day & J. Antonakis (Eds.), *The nature of leadership* (2nd ed., pp. 289–330). SAGE.

Von Au, C. (2016). Paradigmenwechsel in der Führung: Traditionelle Führungsansätze, Wandel und Leadership heute. In C. von Au (Ed.), *Wirksame und nachhaltige Führungsansätze: System, Beziehung, Haltung und Individualität* (pp. 1–42). Springer.

von Rosenstiel, L. (2014). Grundlagen der Führung. In L. von Rosenstiel, E. Regnet, & M. Domsch (Eds.), *Führung von Mitarbeitern: Handbuch für erfolgreiches Personalmanagement* (pp. 3–28, 7th ed.). Schäffer-Poeschl.

Vroom, V. H., & Jago, A. G. (2007). The role of situation in leadership. *American Psychologist, 62*, 17–24.

Vroom, V. H., & Yetton, P. W. (1973). *Leadership and decision-making*. University of Pittsburgh.

Wald, P. M. (2014). Virtuelle Führung. In R. Lang & I. Rybnikova (Eds.), *Aktuelle Führungstheorien und -konzepte* (pp. 355–386). Springer. https://doi.org/10.1007/978-3-8349-3729-2_13

Weber, M. (1976). *Wirtschaft und Gesellschaft: Grundriss der verstehenden Soziologie* (5th ed.). Mohr-Siebeck.

Weibler, J. (2016): *Personalführung* (3rd ed.). de Gruyter, München.

Werther, S. (2013). *Geteilte Führung - Ein Paradigmenwechsel in der Führungsforschung*. Springer Gabler. https://doi.org/10.1007/978-3-658-03580-8_1

Yukl, G. (1994). *Leadership in organizations* (3rd ed.). Prentice Hall.

Zaleznik, A. (1977). Managers and leaders: Are they different? *Harvard Business Review, 55*(3), 67–78.

Chapter 3
Leadership Research and Its Application to Social Work Practice

3.1 Dimensions of Leadership[1]

Peter G. Northouse (2016, p. 6–15) understands leadership as "a process whereby an individual influences a group of individuals to achieve a common goal". With regard to the differentiation of leadership approaches, the same author and later research (e.g. Arnold, 2019) suggest the following distinction:

- *Leadership can be understood either as shaped by certain personality traits or as a process*: Leaders potentially possess different personality traits, such as charisma, emotional intelligence, extraversion and other skills and abilities that help distinguish them from "non-leaders". According to this view, leadership is seen from the perspective of the leader. To simplify somewhat, it is mostly about their "innate" talents and qualities. In contrast, leadership can also be understood as a process of interaction between the leader and led. Leadership, according to the latter perspective, can then be observed in the real behaviour of leaders in relation to those being led and is understood as a lifelong learning process.
- *Leadership can be attributed to or arise from leadership action*: A person can become a leader by being given an appropriate position or assigned a specific function within an organisation. In this case, leadership is associated with a role. However, leadership can also be demonstrated when a person – regardless of their function – is perceived and claimed by others as an influential member of a group or organisation (cf. e.g. Fröse, 2015, pp. 254–322).
- *Leadership is always also connected with the processing of power relations*: Successful leaders are more or less engaged in influencing the actions, beliefs and attitudes of others. Power is an essential aspect of the specific relationship between a leader and led and should not be viewed negatively per se. Power is

---

[1] This is an overview of the discussion of leadership research that updates and expands previous reviews by, e.g. Arnold (2017, 2019), Fröse (2015) and Fröse et al. (2019).

distributed according to position (to legitimise, sanction or reward others) or through personal influence, e.g. through opinion leadership, expertise or knowledge and information sharing.
- *Leadership not only is a process of interaction but also creates cohesion and a bond within and between individuals and groups*: Leadership opens up opportunities for several individuals to work together and develop a common organisational culture. It is however not uncommon to observe the opposite phenomenon, that leadership also presupposes a compulsive alignment with the goals of the leader or organisation. Thus, the leadership process also creates a compulsion to change and influence employee behaviour through recognition and sanctioning.
- *Leadership can also be seen as an activity*: Leaders bring about change and transformation within organisations by setting objectives to which people in organisations align themselves, thereby motivating and inspiring them in their actions. In terms of managing an organisation, leaders provide order and consistency, e.g. through the various management tasks of planning and budgeting, organising and controlling and problem-solving.

3.2 Leadership as a Context of Interaction and Power

In the evolution of the concept of leadership, various semantic differentiations could be observed in the management research literature. From the perspective of interaction theory, Bass and Stogdill (1990) defined leadership in their *Handbook of Leadership* as an:

> interaction between two or more members of a group that often involves a structuring or restructuring of the situation and the perceptions and expectations of the members. Leaders are agents of change – persons whose acts affect other people more than other people's acts affect them. (p. 19–20)

Accordingly, leadership is not only focused on staff development and the corresponding management of expectations towards those being led but is also to be seen as a communicative and goal-oriented action between leader and employees related to the changing framework conditions in an organisation. Burns (1978) points out that leadership is always embedded in a power-related interaction context:

> Leadership over human beings is exercised when persons with certain motives and purposes mobilise, in competition or conflict with others, institutional, political, psychological, and other resources so as to arouse, engage, and satisfy the motives of followers. (p. 18)

Put differently, leadership is not free of domination and power interests, which can vary widely for leaders and followers: Leaders take the initiative and bear responsibility in the leadership process as well as articulate the desires, goals and motives of those being led. Followers are "convinced" by the leader and their actions are influenced or changed by leaders (Burns, 1978, pp. 20–21). This influence can ultimately take place in different ways, as already described in a similar perspective in the classical humanistic leadership theories, e.g. in the *XY theory* according to McGregor

(1966). Broadly speaking, this theory differentiates between theory X for disinterested and unmotivated employees on the one hand and theory Y (positive attitude towards others) for committed employees who need to be motivated on the other. In contrast to theory Y, employees of theory X are lethargic, incapable of self-direction and autonomous work behaviour (Kopelman et al., 2008, p. 255).

As noted above in the distinction between leadership and management concepts (see Chap. 2), the goals and tasks of leaders usually go far beyond the functions of managers. According to Bennis (1989, pp. 12–13), leaders can be regarded as conceptualists who contribute to the development of sense-making, trust-building and, through their charisma, empowerment and participation in the company. From a critical point of view, it can be argued that even more important than hierarchy in leadership is the continuous work of trust between leaders and led as well as the acceptance of permanent change. According to Calás and Simrcich (1997), leadership is characterised by a questioning of the basic assumptions of the organisation; a questioning attitude is always part of one's own role reflection, which is ultimately also taken into account in the systemic-organisational approaches described below.

3.3 Systemic-Organisational Leadership Theories

Systems-theoretical approaches have opened up new perspectives in leadership research and have brought about a partial emancipation from classical approaches, which are more strongly based on the charisma of leaders and directed towards transformational approaches. According to Avery (2004, pp. 146–149), leadership behaviour focuses on communicating visions, values for change and finding meaning. Due to the diversity and varying complexity of situations, not every situation can necessarily always be considered controllable.

The systems-theoretical understanding also has a meaning for the inner life of organisations. In this regard, Simon (2015) describes various characteristics of organisations as social systems, which ultimately also shape everyday leadership (Arnold, 2017, pp. 32–34): (1) It is in the nature of organisations that the people acting in them are interchangeable mainly because they are able to form enduring patterns of action, such as defined process flows and concepts or even complex services. (2) Organisations are themselves understood as acting entities, with their members being understood as "necessary elements of the environment" (Simon, 2015, p. 14; transl. MA) of their organisation. Multiple affiliations are included here. (3) In terms of the complexity reduction capacity of social systems, the "decoupling of person and action" and the "formation of patterns based on the division of labour" (Simon, 2015, p. 14; transl. MA) in organisations can organise complex (problem-solving) processes more effectively and based on the division of labour, as is often not possible by individuals alone. (4) In organisations, there is always an attempt to form changeable and processual structures that "constantly threaten to fall apart" and that therefore "must be constantly rebuilt" (Simon, 2015, p. 16; transl. MA). (5) Organisations act through individuals:

> The real point in attributing actions to organisations is that organisational activities are social, not solitary, and that these activities are so precisely defined that a variety of individuals can contribute the ingredients necessary to maintain the pattern. The pattern can withstand a change of staff as well as some degree of change in the actual behaviour that individuals contribute. It is the performance of the pattern passing through the contributions of interchangeable individuals that distinguishes organisations from other collectivities. (Weick, 1979, pp. 53–54, as cited in Simon, 2015, p. 17; transl. MA)

In this context, communication is also understood as the link between the different (sub)systems of the organisation and to the outside world and also has a pairing, connecting and associating function between the actors within a system and between the subsystems respectively in and for an organisation. (6) Organisations can be understood as "autopoietic" (Greek *autos* for "self" and *poiesis* for "creative activity, work"): Organisations create and develop quasi-organically by (self-)organising themselves.

Organisational approaches to leadership theory are directly linked to the conceptual model of the learning organisation according to Senge (1990). This concept focuses on the collective learning process and knowledge management in the organisation which is coherent with the systemic approach described above. Leadership is thus always involved in the continuous change of the organisation, where leadership can have different functional characteristics (e.g. as "creatives" or "designers" of the system; Senge, 1990, p. 341). Senge also distinguishes between different roles, such as *steward:ess* as servant-leaders who develop and communicate narratives in the organisation, motivate and mobilise others (Senge, 1990, pp. 345–346), while the role of the *teacher*, who knows the system inside out, can be understood as that of a translator for the messages announced by the steward:ess (Senge, 1990, p. 356). Senge (1990) also points out that leadership should always be seen as a game between collective and individual goal fulfilment:

> One of the paradoxes of leadership in learning organisations is that it is both collective and highly individual. Although the responsibilities of leadership are diffused among men and women throughout the organisation, the responsibilities come only as a result of individual choice. Only through choice does an individual come to be the steward of a larger vision. Only through choice does an individual come to practice the learning disciplines. Being in a supportive environment can help, but it does not obviate the need for choice. Learning organizations can only be built by individuals who put their life spirit into the task. It is our choices that focus the spirit. The choice, as is always the case, is yours. (p. 360)

If this theoretical approach is taken further, leadership focuses more on group dynamics, teamwork and leadership interaction. In addition, the institutional-structural framework conditions, social framework conditions and sociocultural networks are included in the approach (Fröse, 2015, p. 264). A critical objection to Senge's (1990) understanding of collective leadership is that when responsibility is shifted from individual tasks and goals to the group or team level, group dynamics are also influenced (both favourably and unfavourably), provided that interests and goals have been translated accordingly. Furthermore, a cultural translation and adaptation must also take place in the implementation of this approach. According to Senge et al. (2004), leaders should develop a "personal mastery" in the sense of the Far Eastern traditions, true to the motto: "All understanding is preceded by self-knowledge – as an important prerequisite for leaders" (Fröse et al., 2019, p. 14, transl. MA). "If you want to be a leader, you have to be a real human being. You must recognise the true meaning of life before you can become a great leader. You must understand yourself first" (Master Nan, as cited in Senge et al., 2004, p. 186).

In this context, Bohm (1980, p. 29), Zohar (1997, pp. 142–143), Senge (1990, p. 241) and Wheatley (2007, p. 115) emphasise the relevance of dialogue work in the leadership process, which contributes to organisational learning. In other systemic-organisational approaches to leadership, the focus is rather on developing the qualities of interactional relationships in organisations. In Wheatley's (2007) ecosystemic approach, trust, relationships and interdependencies between the members of an organisation as well as their ability to engage in dialogue are considered more important than a constant confrontation with "external" conditions (e.g. competition in social markets): "If you are going to be a leader of a living system very different skills are going to be required of you: participation, learning, perceptive realities, curiosity, connectedness, and the ability to find meaningful order in messes" (Wheatley, 2007, p. 115). Stacey and Griffin (2005, pp. 10–11) also see social recognition as an absolute prerequisite for the development and implementation of leadership: "The leader is as much formed by the recognition of the group as he or she forms the group in his or her recognition of the others". In his integral theory, Wilber (2000) further points out that leadership must be considered at the individual and collective level as well as from an internal and external perspective: In this context, the *individual-internal perspective* (leadership is enabled/influenced by personality development, reflection, transfer of expertise and methods) and the *collective perspective* (leadership plays a role at the conscious/visible and unconscious/invisible level of organisational culture and can have both a supportive and obstructive) appear to be particularly relevant (Wilber, 2000, pp. 62–64).

3.4 Adaptive Leadership

In more recent approaches to adaptive leadership, systemic, interactionist and organisational principles are increasingly integrated with one other (cf. for an overview Arnold, 2019). A common underlying assumption of these approaches is that today's leaders, regardless of industry or organisational form, must remain flexible and willing to adapt to ever-changing situations to maintain their effectiveness and productivity (Yukl & Mahsud, 2010, p. 82). Furthermore, these approaches are based on the notion that successful leaders are tied to close collaboration with others in everything they do, especially when dynamic work environments challenge established leadership structures and leadership processes can be assumed to be fluid or agile (DeRue, 2011, pp. 130–131).

In addition, several studies have analysed adaptive responsiveness to changes in employees' perceptions of leadership interactions. For example, Voirin, Akremi and Vandenberghe (2010, p. 716) show that adaptive leadership is intertwined with the establishment and development of volatile work environments or organisational cultures, which is related to the fact that actions of leaders in an organisation have a direct impact on the actions and attitudes of their followers. In general, anticipating and responding to expected changes within organisations is described as an essential component of adaptive leadership (Hogan, 2008).

Other research has produced similar findings. In social and human service organisations, adaptive leadership can be understood as an extension of cooperation between existing team members, with particular emphasis on the influence of leaders on team dynamics (Ospina & Foldy, 2010, pp. 293–294). Moreover, adaptive leadership is not an entirely new phenomenon but combines a variety of principles, approaches and methods discussed elsewhere in the human resource management literature (Hall et al., 2009), including, for example, the "zone of indifference" (Barnard, 1938, p. 167) as well as the systemic view and transformational aspects of motivation, sense-making and mobilising staff in the context of teamwork (Northouse, 2016, pp. 259–260).

The development of adaptive skills and abilities of leaders and staff in the process of adaptive leadership has been explored in numerous studies: For example, workplace interactions more often lead to positive change, which can be observed in performance feedback and behaviour change (Nelson et al., 2010, pp. 139–140). In addition, several studies have demonstrated the transferability and applicability of adaptive leadership in various industries, such as the military (Cojacar, 2011; Wallace II, 2018), medicine (Haeusler, 2010), mental health (Gonçalves, 2017) and academic library (Wong & Chan, 2018), health professions education (McKimm et al., 2022) and (higher) education (Daly & Chrispeels, 2007; Norris, 2018). The adaptive leadership approach can be applied to almost any organisation and environment, including, for example, not-for-profit organisations, schools, charities, religious institutions and healthcare. All of these organisations face complex challenges and strategies that require consistent stakeholder management and a working through of multi-rationality and hybridity (Arnold, 2017). Adaptive leadership has also been implemented at the organisational level to upskill community school leaders and the leadership competencies of principals (Chace, 2013; Guilleux, 2010).

One challenge in implementing this leadership approach is to better understand the specific behaviours of all stakeholders involved in the respective work context (Adams et al., 2013). This has proven to be particularly important in diaconal settings. For example, due to declining membership in many religious communities around the world, adaptive leadership is seen as a necessary component to further develop work in denominationally supported social welfare organisations (Muir, 2017). Indeed, some of the diaconal literature focuses on describing principles, methods and approaches for implementing adaptive leadership in diaconal settings (see, among others, Arnold et al., 2017).

According to Heifetz (1994, p. 57), leaders possess authority in everyday organisational life and ultimately bear a responsibility that is expected from the group of followers. However, this is influenced by their reciprocal relationship. A group can have power, which can also challenge the authority of the leader. According to this view, leadership is not necessarily only an assumed role, function or personality trait, but can always be understood as an ongoing activity ("doing") to initiate, realise and control organisational development processes: As goals, tasks and decisions in social organisations are often "dependent on governmental and sectoral objectives, purposes, resources and needs", and leaders are seen as "organisational designers" (Fröse et al., 2019, p. 15; transl. MA), this also entails a specific understanding of the governance and leadership of these organisations. The *Practice of Adaptive Leadership* (Heifetz et al., 2009), in realising the underlying participatory understanding of leadership, generally proves to be a key to the successful governance of social organisations, "especially when leaders mobilise their followers for so-called adaptive challenges so that they can move forward in their field of work and action and seek solutions together" (Fröse et al., 2019, p. 15; transl. MA).

Finally, Boal and Schultz (2007) emphasise that in complex and adaptive systems, leadership at a strategic level may become redundant:

> We suggest that strategic leadership pushes organisations to the 'edge of chaos' and out of stasis; without it no significant change can emerge. Strategy leadership promotes 'strange attraction' in organisations, providing balance between the inertia of Weberian-style bureaucracy and anarchy, resulting in the ordered and fluid responsiveness of innovative and creative organisation. In practice, strategic leaders achieve balance in a number of different ways; as part of complex adaptive systems, they are agents that guide the interactions of other agents and transfer particular kinds of resource flows. Specifically, we argue that in creating complex adaptive organisational systems, strategic leaders channel knowledge (by altering interaction patterns) about organisational identity and vision (by promoting dialogue and organisational narratives). (p. 411)

3.5 Conclusion

Leadership, as has been shown, can be described by various dimensions, including personality traits, leadership actions or styles, power relations, group dynamic factors and activities. It is also associated with ethical values and is closely intertwined with HRD issues, always balancing individual and organisational goals, expectations and strategies. In the future, the discussion of power issues in their various facets must be intensified in the context of leadership, especially in the context of different management levels of leadership, the quality of decision-making processes and the organisational psychological barriers to action (e.g. in the MAK model) (cf. Rehwaldt, 2019). Systemic approaches also suggest that leadership as a collaborative behaviour or contribution to cooperation has a specific significance for all levels and in all places in organisations (on micro-, meso- and macro-level). Leadership can be translated or understood as a function, position, role or activity. Leaders and led are in a dynamic relationship with one another in the organisation, or, in other words, all those involved in an organisation find themselves in a mutually influencing network communication (cf. St. Gallen Management Model of the 3rd generation; Rüegg-Stürm, 2004). Finally, more recent approaches and theories of transformational, adaptive and collective leadership emphasise that organisations can also be steered by sense-making and storytelling and develop their own learning cultures (Ancona, 2012).

References

Adams, J. A., Bailey, D. E., Jr., Anderson, R. A., & Galanos, A. N. (2013). Adaptive leadership: A novel approach for family decision making. *Journal of Palliative Medicine, 16*(3), 326–329. https://doi.org/10.1089/jpm.2011.0406

Ancona, D. (2012). Sensemaking: Framing and acting in the unknown. In S. A. Snook, N. Nohria, & K. Rakesh (Eds.), *The handbook for teaching leadership: Knowing, doing, and being* (pp. 3–19). SAGE.

Arnold, M. (2017). Diakonische Praxis und ihre Gestaltung in Organisationen. In M. Arnold, D. Bonchino-Demmler, R. Evers, M. Hussmann, & U. Liedke (Eds.), *Perspektiven diakonischer Profilentwicklung: Ein Arbeitsbuch am Beispiel von Einrichtungen der Diakonie in Sachsen* (pp. 28–48). EVA.

Arnold, M. (2019). Leading change in human service Organisations in the 21st century. In M. W. Fröse, B. Naake, & M. Arnold (Eds.), *Führung und Organisation: Neue Entwicklungen im Management der Sozial- und Gesundheitswirtschaft* (pp. 159–174). Springer. https://doi.org/10.1007/978-3-658-24193-3_8

Arnold, M., Bonchino-Demmler, D., & Hußmann, M. (2017). Einblicke: Die empirische Untersuchung »Perspektiven Diakonischer Profilentwicklung am Beispiel von Einrichtungen der Diakonie in Sachsen«. In M. Arnold, D. Bonchino-Demmler, R. Evers, M. Hußmann, & U. Liedke, (Eds.), Perspektiven diakonischer Profilbildung: Ein Arbeitsbuch am Beispiel von Einrichtungen der Diakonie in Sachsen (pp. 253–268). EVA.

Avery, G. (2004). *Understanding leadership: Paradigms and cases.* SAGE.

Barnard, C. I. (1938). *The functions of the executive.* Harvard University Press.

Bass, B. M., & Stogdill. (1990). *Handbook of leadership: Theory, research, and managerial applications.* Free Press.

Bennis, W. (1989). *On becoming a leader.* Basic Books.

Boal, K. B., & Schultz, P. L. (2007). Storytelling, time, and evolution: The role of strategic leadership in complex adaptive systems. *The Leadership Quarterly, 18*(4), 411–428. https://doi.org/10.1016/j.leaqua.2007.04.008

Bohm, D. (1980). *Wholeness and the implicate order.* Routledge.

Burns, J. M. (1978). *Leadership.* Harper & Row.

Calás, M. B., & Simrcich, L. (1997). Voicing seduction to silence leadership. In K. Grint (Ed.), *Leadership: Classical, contemporary, and critical approaches* (pp. 338–379). Oxford University Press.

Chace, S. (2013). Learning leadership: A case study on influences of a leadership training program on the practice of one group of urban school superintendents. [Unpublished doctoral dissertation]. Teachers College Columbia University.

Cojacar, W. (2011). Adaptive leadership in military decision process. Defense technical information center. *Military Review, 91*(6), 29–34. https://www.armyupress.army.mil/Portals/7/military-review/Archives/English/MilitaryReview_20120630MC_art007.pdf

Daly, A., & Chrispeels, J. (2007). A question of trust. *Leadership and Policy in Schools, 1*, 30–63. https://doi.org/10.1080/15700760701655508

DeRue, S. (2011). Adaptive leadership theory. *Research in Organisational Behavior, 31*, 125–150. https://doi.org/10.1016/j.riob.2011.09.007

Fröse, M. (2015). *Transformationen in ›sozialen‹ Organisationen: Verborgene Komplexitäten. Ein Entwurf.* Würzburg: Ergon.

Fröse, M. W., Naake, B., & Arnold, M. (2019). Quo Vadis - leadership und organisation. In M. W. Fröse, B. Naake, & M. Arnold (Eds.), *Führung und Organisation: Neue Entwicklungen im Management der Sozial- und Gesundheitswirtschaft* (pp. 1–30). Springer. https://doi.org/10.1007/978-3-658-24193-3_1

Gonçalves, M. (2017). Adaptive leadership in the promotion of youth mental health. *International Journal of Clinical Neurosciences and Mental Health, 4*, 1–6. https://doi.org/10.21035/ijcnmh.2017.4.1

References

Guilleux, F. (2010). *A development perspective on leadership education of aspiring principals.* [Unpublished doctoral dissertation]. University of Pittsburgh.

Haeusler, J. (2010). Medicine needs adaptive leadership. *Physician Executive, 36*(2), 12–15.

Hall, M., Hall, C., Andrade, L., & Drake, B. (2009). Strategic human resource management: The evolution of the field. *Human Resource Management Review, 19*(2), 64–85. https://doi.org/10.1016/j.hrmr.2009.01.002

Heifetz, R. A. (1994). *Leadership without easy answers.* Belknap Press.

Heifetz, R. A., Grashow, A., & Linsky, M. (2009). *The practice of adaptive leadership: Tools and tactics for changing your organisation and the world.* Harvard Business Press.

Hogan, T. (2008). The adaptive leadership maturity model. *Organisational Development Journal, 26*(1), 55–61.

Kopelman, R. E., Prottas, D. J., & Davis, A. L. (2008). Douglas McGregor's theory X and Y: Toward a construct-valid measure. *Journal of Managerial Issues, 20*(2), 255–271. http://www.jstor.org/stable/40604607

McGregor, D. (1966). *Leadership and motivation.* MIT Press.

McKimm, J., Ramani, S., Forrest, K., Bishop, J., Findyartini, A., Mills, C., Hassanien, M., Al-Hayani, A., Jones, P., Nadarajah, V. D., & Radu, G. (2022). *Adaptive leadership during challenging times: Effective strategies for health professions educators: AMEE guide no. 148.* Medical teacher, pp. 1–11. https://doi.org/10.1080/0142159X.2022.2057288.

Muir, S. D. (2017). *Why do they stay? Lay church leaders and the demands of institutional change.* [Doctoral dissertation]. University of Toronto. http://hdl.handle.net/1807/77646

Nelson, J. K., Zaccaro, S. J., & Herman, J. L. (2010). Strategic information provision and experiential variety as tools for developing adaptive leadership skills. *Consulting Psychology Journal: Practice and Research, 62*(2), 131–142. https://doi.org/10.1037/a0019989

Norris, S. E. (2018). An adaptive leadership approach to adult learning and Organisational research. In V. Wang & T. G. Reio Jr. (Eds.), *Handbook of research on innovative techniques, trends, and analysis for optimized research methods* (pp. 99–114). IGI Global. https://doi.org/10.4018/978-1-5225-5164-5.ch007

Northouse, P. G. (2016). *Leadership: Theory and practice* (7th ed.). SAGE.

Ospina, S., & Foldy, E. (2010). Building bridges from the margins. *The Leadership Quarterly, 21*(2), 292–307. https://doi.org/10.1016/j.leaqua.2010.01.008

Rehwaldt, R. (2019). Hinter den Kulissen – Narzissmus, Macht und Sozialisation als Handlungsbarrieren für Glück in Organisationen. In M. W. Fröse, B. Naake, & M. Arnold (Eds.), *Führung und Organisation: Neue Entwicklungen im Management der Sozial- und Gesundheitswirtschaft* (pp. 197–216). Springer. https://doi.org/10.1007/978-3-658-24193-3_10

Rüegg-Stürm, J. (2004). Das neue St. Galler Management–Modell. In R. Dubs (Ed.), *Einführung in die Managementlehre* (pp. 65–141). Haupt.

Senge, P. M. (1990). *The fifth discipline: The art and practice of the learning organization.* Doubleday.

Senge, P., Scharmer, C. O., Jaworski, J., & Flowers, B. S. (2004). *Presence: Human purpose and the field of the future.* Currency.

Simon, F. B. (2015). *Einführung in die systemische Organisationstheorie* (5th ed.). Carl Auer.

Stacey, R., & Griffin, D. (Eds.). (2005). *A complexity perspective on researching organizations: Taking experience seriously.* Routledge.

Voirin, A., Akremi, A., & Vandenberghe, C. (2010). A multilevel model of transformational leadership and adaptive performance and the moderating role of climate for innovation. *Group & Organisation Management, 35*(6), 699–726. https://doi.org/10.1177/1059601110390833

Wallace II, L. T. (2018). *Adaptive leadership in high-stress occupations: Applications to the military* (Publication no. 10745536) [doctoral dissertation, northcentral university]. ProQuest dissertations and theses global.

Weick, K. E. (1979). *Der Prozeß des Organisierens.* Frankfurt a. M.

Wheatley, M. J. (2007). A new paradigm for a new leadership. In R. A. Couto (Ed.), *Reflections on leadership* (pp. 105–115). University Press of America.

Wilber, K. (2000). *Integral psychology: Consciousness, Spirit, psychology, therapy*. Shambala.

Wong, G. K. W., & Chan, D. L. H. (2018). Adaptive leadership in academic libraries. *Library Management, 39*(1/2), 106–115. https://doi.org/10.1108/LM-06-2017-0060

Yukl, G., & Mahsud, R. (2010). Why flexible and adaptive leadership is essential. *Consulting Psychology Journal: Practice and Research, 62*(2), 81–93. https://doi.org/10.1037/a0019835

Zohar, D. (1997). *Rewiring the corporate brain: Using the new science to rethink how we structure and Lead organizations*. Berrett-Koehler.

Chapter 4
Transformation of Leadership and Collaboration in Human Service Organisations

4.1 Context and Framework of New Leadership Concepts

Newer leadership approaches and concepts have developed primarily against the backdrop of the following framework conditions. These include in particular the digital transformation and technological change under VUCA conditions (VUCA for *v*olatility, *u*ncertainty, *c*omplexity and *a*mbiguity), which poses new challenges for all organisations as well as all forms of education and knowledge work (e.g. Mack et al., 2015). Leadership can therefore no longer be conceived without digitalisation. In recent approaches to organisational theory, the view that interaction between leaders and led as well as the design of working conditions and organisational culture in social and human service organisations is particularly challenged by the so-called digital transformation has gradually gained acceptance (cf. Arnold, 2021). In recent times, and not just because of the COVID-19 pandemic, and cooperation via geographically and temporally distributed structures, the lack of direct contact results in a rethinking of the work environment. Traditional leadership approaches, which presuppose direct and hierarchical relationships between leaders and led, seem rather unsuitable for these types of work-related contexts and conditions. Many small- and medium-sized organisations are still confronted with a change that often receives too little if any attention: the generational shift. When the company founders, owners, visionaries and drivers of organisational development retire or otherwise part ways with their company and a new generation of managers with at times different values, views and expectations takes over or continues to run the company, together with Lippold (2019, p. 29; transl. MA), we may ask: "How can it be possible to live an intergenerational, better generation-bridging communication or corporate culture?"

Many of the (post)modern leadership approaches can be classified in the so-called dynamic-situational management school ("dynamic engagement" cf. Grodsky, n.d.). Generally, these are theoretically and empirically based concepts as well as practical approaches that take the dynamics and changeability of organisations as a starting point and emphasise certain factors depending on the theoretical perspective. In the management and design of organisations today, methods and instruments are needed that allow dealing with constant change. For example, in project management, a fixed project plan cannot be assumed. In the sense of agile management, work systems are increasingly to be organised in such a way that changes are not seen as disruptive factors, but rather as catalyst for optimising the production of customer- or client-oriented products and services (e.g. Scrum technique, adaptive leadership approach). Against this background, various conclusions or theses can be derived that provide an insight into and outlook on the objectives of newer leadership approaches (Arnold, 2022a, transl. MA):

- *"Stakeholders form a network of partners internally and with the system environment.* All stakeholders, who have a relationship with the institution, are interconnected within and outside the institution. This must be continuously taken into account and included within the framework of (stakeholder) management.
- *Achieving goals includes moral and ethical responsibility towards those involved.* Decision-making processes and their results are usually not value-free. In management and performance tasks, moral-ethical issues must always be taken into account. For example, ethical case discussions/analyses in the context of socio-educational or nursing work reflect on how the work is provided, which values and convictions as well as limitations of care and treatment exist.
- *Networks, internationalisation and clients are part of an institution.* In the course of globalisation, we find ourselves in more networked contexts. Not only new technologies but also international networks enable new forms of cooperation. Multi-, trans- and interculturality increasingly play an important role in all fields of work, and not only in migration social work.
- *Organisational structures have to be constantly adapted and reinvented.* Changes within the institution and in the environment of an organisation often also require an adaptation, development and reinvention of structures, processes and organisational culture. Organisational theory approaches must provide answers to this (cf. model of adaptive leadership above). Organisational development and human resource development should not be seen as two separate and detached areas.
- *Organisations need to respond to societal changes.* As already indicated, organisations have to react to constantly changing conditions in the environment. Such changes concern, for example, amendments to laws, competitive pressure or deterioration of the cost structure. Against this background, change management approaches are becoming increasingly important.
- *Increasing importance of quality management.* In management practice and theory, as well as in the social and economic sciences in general, various theories, models, and approaches as well as methods have been developed on how to ensure quality assurance in organisations. This involves standardisation of processes, insurance of professional quality and enhancement of quality from both structural, processual, and outcome perspectives".

In the following subsections, some of the most extensively studied approaches, concepts and theories will be presented as examples of the numerous new leadership approaches that support the transformation of processes, strategies, structures and cultures through leadership and collaboration in social work and human service institutions in the future: (Sect. 4.2) adaptive leadership, (Sect. 4.3) digital/virtual leadership and (Sect. 4.4) agile leadership.

4.2 The Practice of Adaptive Leadership[1]

The model of "adaptive leadership" (cf. Heifetz et al., 2009) has gained increasing importance in recent years due to its relevance also for social work organisations when dealing with so-called adaptive challenges. This model focuses on adaptations that people in organisation have to cope with in response to changes that (1) require organisational learning as well as challenge and replace existing management practices, (2) call for the development of new skills and competencies and facilitate staff development through new situations and (3) mobilise staff to change their behaviour, values and attitudes in uncertain situations. This approach involves a *systemic perspective* (complex problems with many perspectives), a *biological perspective* (people in an organisation need to adapt to internal and external environments), a *service orientation* (diagnosing problems and prescribing solutions through teamwork) and a *psychotherapeutic perspective* (understanding people's needs and helping them identify situations in which they feel uncomfortable) (Northouse, 2016, pp. 259–260). The model includes three phases: identifying the problem, developing solutions, or finding learning opportunities and implementing change. Adaptive leadership is a complex leadership theory (Uhl-Bien et al., 2007) that describes a dynamic process and promotes, among other things, problem-solving and creative skills. It is not tied to a single person or specific action.

In this model, leadership is not seen as a role, function or position, but as a continuous activity involving all stakeholders within the organisation. In other words, leadership practice is an "activity to mobilise people to address so-called adaptive challenges" (Heifetz et al., 2009, p. 76). This approach is not manager-centred but employee-centred and is dedicated to the interactions between employees and managers. Accordingly, leadership must be viewed in a broader context (Heifetz et al., 2009, pp. 74–75): People possess leadership that addresses problems openly to seize new opportunities and deal with the inevitable changes in prevailing attitudes, behaviours and beliefs. Adaptive leadership mobilises all stakeholders in the organisation and prepares them for change. Employees often take on responsibilities and challenges that go far beyond what is expected of them; they are able to work independently and with purpose. In this context, leadership cannot be equated with authority. The following figure contains a visual representation of the main

---

[1] This section summarises and updates research previously presented in Arnold (2019).

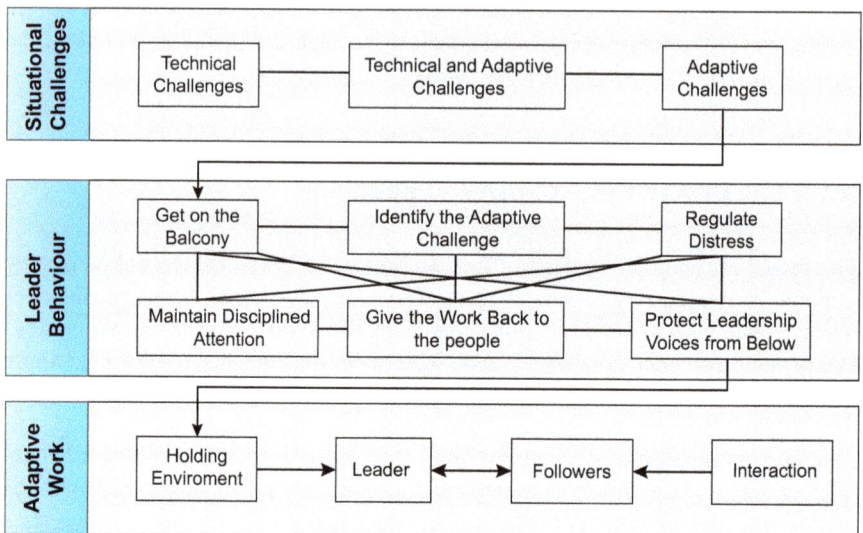

Fig. 4.1 Model of adaptive leadership according to Heifetz (1994). (Adapted from Northouse, 2016, p. 261 (Used with permission of SAGE College, from *Leaders*hip by Peter G. Northouse, © 2015; permission conveyed through Copyright Clearance Center, Inc.))

components of the model, which systematically addresses situational challenges, leadership behaviour and adaptive work (see Fig. 4.1).

4.2.1 Situation Challenges

Management decisions are usually linked to different situational conditions and challenges. This is illustrated in Fig. 4.1 on top level. These challenges and problems in everyday management can be either "technical" or "adaptive" in nature or a combination of both (cf. Heifetz et al., 2009, pp. 76–83). Technical challenges, which can be clearly identified and overcome with known solutions, can typically be implemented using the existing expertise of managers, with the help of standard operating procedures and rules, and by a decision of the person in charge. Additionally, adaptive challenges also frequently characterise everyday leadership. Such challenges are gaps between existing know-how on the current *actual* state and the desired future *target* state, the achievement of which requires learning and change; in these situations, there is no clearly defined path to a solution. This increasingly challenges managers to encourage and enable other staff with their support to develop new ways of thinking and working. For example, if a patient needs to stop smoking due to illness, they need to adopt new priorities and habits. Adaptation challenges are often linked not only to the person but also to the systemic context. For this reason, adaptive leaders need to analyse the interests and positions of stakeholders and find out how people can learn in the process of change. Therefore, problem-solving always involves the whole team or all relevant stakeholders. Addressing adaptive challenges requires a certain attitude from the employees: The employees and the challenges they face in the organisation are both the problem and the solution (Heifetz et al., 2009, p. 20). An adaptive challenge requires employees to distinguish between what is useful and necessary and what is dispensable or can be changed within the organisational culture. In the context of constant organisational change, the task consists of holding on to basic values, beliefs and norms, but also to occasionally break away from outdated and traditional patterns as well as to learn something new (Heifetz et al., 2009, p. 79). In other words, adaptive leaders are needed who accept the harsh reality, urge for change and can deal with employees' experiences of loss so that (further) development of their skills and competences becomes possible. Employees are encouraged and "mobilised" in the process of adaptation and change to make tough decisions on occasion and strengthen their commitment and trust in the organisation. From a practical point of view, it is always necessary to ask: What is the real problem, what is being ignored by everyone, what are the hopes and fears of the people in the institution, what are the opportunities and risks associated with change, and what lessons need to be learned to achieve the desired state?

4.2.2 Leadership Behaviour

As shown at the middle level of Fig. 4.1, with the help of the six ideal-typical principles and methods of leadership behaviour, leadership success is influenced within the framework of adaptive leadership (cf. summarised Northouse, 2016, pp. 261–273):

1. *Leaders must regularly "go on the balcony"*. This metaphor means that meta-observations and reflections should be part of daily leadership practice. This method of observation helps, for example, to identify work avoidance and dysfunctional routines.
2. *Adaptive leaders must first understand, diagnose and articulate the adaptive framework and only then can they identify support structures to ultimately initiate the learning process*. In this context, Heifetz et al. (2009, pp. 78–87) describe four archetypes of adaptive challenges: (i) "gaps between expressed values and behaviours", (ii) "competing commitments", (iii) "speaking the unspeakable", (iv) "work avoidance" and "staying in the comfort zone".
3. *Adaptive leaders must counter the fears, questions and distresses* of those being led which inevitably arise during change. Leaders should deal with personal distress, discomfort and uncertainty of all involved and create a productive,

creative work environment where people feel safe and guided and where conflicts are resolved.
4. *Adaptive leaders must encourage staff to focus on the hard work that needs to be done to maintain disciplined attention.* It is the responsibility of leaders to encourage and support all employees to do their jobs and to openly address and face inevitable changes.
5. *"Giving the work back to the people"* (Heifetz et al., 2009) means that while adaptive leaders provide direction, employees should also empower themselves to help decide what needs to be changed in the current unstable circumstances to meet the adaptive challenge and solve problems that may have arisen.
6. *To support the work of employees, adaptive leaders should observe closely, listen attentively, remain open to people's ideas, reach out to introverted group members as well as give voice to low-status members, dissenters and minorities.* Leaders should create a work environment that encourages commitment, motivation and identification.

4.2.3 Adaptive Work

The bottom level of Fig. 4.1 refers to adaptive work and describes the "process towards which adaptive leaders direct their work" (Northouse, 2016, pp. 273–274). This often requires experimentation and taking various risks. The timeframe of adaptive work can be quite different from that of technical work: It is well known that it takes time and patience for learning to occur from communication between managers and employees. In particular, learning takes place "within a holding environment where people can feel safe as they confront possible changes in their roles, priorities, and values" (Northouse, 2016, p. 273). Adaptive work always interacts with organisational culture and requires both the clarification of values and the assessment of realities that might challenge the realisation of those values: "The adaptive work in cultures involves both the clarification of values and the assessment of realities that challenge the realisation of those values" (Heifetz et al., 2009, p. 82). Even when competing values lead to conflict, leaders need to maintain a safe work environment and interact with all stakeholders in times of change.

To summarise, this model of leadership challenges leaders to step back from the stage to understand and reflect on the complexity of adaptive challenges and upcoming changes. Leaders need to be able to assess the different technical and adaptive challenges of problems that require authority, expertise or a change in rules and procedures within an organisation. Skills of adaptive leaders should include dealing with adversity, creating a supportive environment rather than giving instructions and supporting, mobilising and empowering people.

4.2.4 Strengths and Weaknesses of the Model

This model has some key advantages and strengths (Northouse, 2016, pp. 275–276) as it:

- *Recognises the dynamic nature of organisations and helps to realise a "process-oriented apporganisational changeroach to leadership"*: in this context, leadership practice is characterised by interactions between leaders and followers in different situations.
- *Fosters employee-centred thinking*: it aims to mobilise stakeholders, it emphasises commitment and motivation to achieve desired goals, and it creates a conducive learning environment.
- *Helps followers deal with complex situations and conflicting values* that develop during .
- *Provides a prescriptive approach* and guidance on what leaders can do.
- *Emphasises the concept of a "safe and structured environment" (holding environment)* to reduce work avoidance, especially when difficulties arise.

Despite its strengths, the model has also received some criticism (e.g. Northouse, 2016, pp. 276–277). While this leadership approach was developed out of a practical context, the theoretical underpinnings are still relatively underdeveloped. The three-factor model described above needs to be broadened to include further dimensions to decisively prove or disprove the empirical relationships between the three factors (situational challenges, leadership behaviour and adaptive work). Additionally, Dugan (2017, p. 141) also sees the "commodification of workers" as problematic, which can be understood as "the extent to which workers are considered fully agentic, vested partners in the process of production or simply tools to augment it". In this way, it could be asked whether workers' dependence (to work in line with the direction of their leaders) will be increased instead of engaging in team and collaborative work (Nelson & Squires, 2017, p. 120). While the model offers a wide range of rules and guidelines, it lacks specificity and conceptual clarity. Finally, the model does not include a moral or ethical dimension, especially for situations where the achievement of a goal may conflict with the values of the organisation (e.g. change does not always lead to improved conditions); moreover, the model does not address how exactly to account for development of "sense-making" in the organisation.

4.3 Digital Leadership[2]

4.3.1 Digitalisation in Social and Human Services

Increasing digitalisation is affecting all areas of life and society as a whole, caused by advances in information technology as well as disruptive and innovative business models that go hand in hand with automation, flexibilisation and individualisation. Brennen and Kreiss (2016, pp. 1–2) define "digitalisation as the material process of transforming analogue information streams into digital bits" and "digitalisation as the way in which many areas of social life are restructured around digital communication and media infrastructures". In contrast, digital business transformation (DBT) refers to an innovation process of a company in itself to digitise tasks and processes: DBT is the "process of reinventing a business to digitise operations and formulate extended supply chain relationships. The DBT leadership challenge is about reenergizing businesses that may already be successful to capture the full potential of information technology across the total supply chain" (Bowersox et al., 2005, pp. 22–23). The most important aspects related to digitalisation are summarised here: (1) changes are happening in all parts of society through digital technologies; (2) it refers to new challenges in capturing, analysing and implementing actions; (3) it is linked to the digital economy; and (4) digitalisation takes place in processes and strategies across the entire value chain.

Educational and social institutions are increasingly challenged by digital transformation. These challenges are directly related to the integration of digital technologies, concepts and strategies in almost all areas of education and social care (Douse & Uys, 2018; Khalid et al., 2018; Kreidenweis, 2018), for example:

1. Advancing digitalisation encompasses changes in structures, processes, strategies of organisations and the entire value chain: new business models for digital platforms in all sectors for intelligent networking, secure data exchange, contract management between provider and customer as well as intelligent analysis of data (digital economy).
2. Service robotics and artificial intelligence aids in elderly care to support people with limited capabilities, e.g. assisted living technologies, intelligent voice recognition and dialogue systems and blockchain technologies in the context of data exchange between state welfare and service providers in the organisation of economic assistance; development, implementation and evaluation of concepts for virtual youth work (so-called cyber street work or virtual youth work 2.0) provide a technological and conceptual basis for future development;
3. Digital participation has become a basic prerequisite for inclusion in society, while economic and demographic factors can exacerbate the digital divide, particularly in disadvantaged communities.

---

[2] The following description of digital leadership is derived from previous publications, e.g. Arnold (2020, 2021).

4. Training, coaching and other support services for educators to develop digital literacy and leadership skills not only for professionals and for managers that go beyond the traditional mindset. Digital literacy involves the ability "to utilise technology to enhance and transform classroom practices and to enrich their professional development and identity" (Hall et al., 2014, p. 5).

Relevant for all organisations and all staff (not just the C-Suite), digital leadership is "a strategic mindset that leverages available resources to improve what we do while anticipating the changes needed to cultivate a school culture focused on efficacy" (Sheninger, 2019, p. XIX). Many educational and social institutions need to develop and enhance digital leadership at different levels (Sheninger, 2019, p. XXI): technology-enhanced learning; developing innovative learning and working environments; professionalising learning processes through personalised learning pathways; using different types of communication strategies and technologies; public relations through storytelling; branding, e.g. through positive use of social media; and using professional learning opportunities. In general, educational and social institutions need to (further) develop leadership in the digital age by adopting a longer-term perspective, "which can only be achieved if a common digital competence base exists and future viable organisational concepts are applied" (p. 104). The following five concept are applied (Kreutzer et al., 2018, p. 105); these include (1) *product ownership* (e.g. linking digitalisation to a clear business strategy), (2) *customer-centric design* (focus on customer relevance, usability and experience), (3) *communication* (gaining support internally and recruiting the best candidates externally), (4) *digital governance* (enabling adaptive strategic planning and identifying opportunities) and (5) *data science* (turning analytics into actionable insights). Before these aspects are explored more closely in Sect. 4.3.3, leadership in the context of digital transformation will be discussed in greater detail.

4.3.2 Leadership in Digital Transformation

Leadership in the context of digital transformation presupposes a distinction between different types of organisational change processes (Porras & Silvers, 1991). On the one hand, the concept of *organisational development* (OD) (synonymous with first-order planned change) can be characterised as follows: In the context of OD, working conditions are partially changed, often with reference to scientific concepts, to provoke behavioural and attitudinal changes in staff. It can also be understood as a response to the internal adaptation needs of developmental and environmental requirements due to changing market conditions. OD leads to a new developmental status quo of an organisation. On the other hand, *organisational transformation* (OT) (synonymous with second-order change) is seen as a paradigmatic change of the entire organisation, e.g. in terms of vision, structures, processes and working conditions, applying scientific concepts. It aims at behavioural and attitudinal changes of staff to shape desired future relationships with(in) the organisational environment. As Porras and Silvers (1991) have pointed out, any kind of change depends on different variables that moderate the change process on at least two levels: the organisational level (e.g. corporate philosophy, working conditions and leadership principles) or the individual level (e.g. personal development of required skills or the introduction of new quality standards).

According to Weick and Quinn (1999), further forms of intervention can be distinguished. First, *episodic change* is a systematic change response that occurs when internal structures and requirements from the system environment have changed. Such organisational change can be characterised, for example, with Kurt Lewin's model of organisational development. Episodic changes concern short-term adjustments. Change agents are responsible for the gradual introduction of new issues and technologies. Critically, episodic change does not allow for long-term developments because it assumes a stable environment and usually involves normative approaches or assumes rational, linear and non-circular change processes (Burnes, 2004). Second, the concept of *continuous change* (Orlikowski, 1996) refers to permanent changes at the level of organisational processes and structures (e.g. adjustments of the product line, according to the demand of market or welfare services). It is characterised by cyclical and long-term process orientation. Change agents must be meaning-makers and translators of change. Third, *planned change* is based on the concept of "think first to act" and requires a stable context, while processes need to be clearly structured. Planned change is a frequently desired concept in change management. Fourth, *improvised change* is closely related to the aforementioned concept of "think and act", but it involves anticipating appropriate changes: When a problem arises, the change agent is responsible for exploiting all opportunities for successful change. Improvised change takes place in typical phases or sequences: anticipating problems, identifying problems, seizing the opportunity and so on.

In human and social service organisations, change management needs to be aligned in terms of different factors that support the initiation of the change process. The "3W model" by Krüger (2009), for example, includes the following components: *need for change* (e.g. in the form of an internal or external situation analysis), *willingness to change* (willingness to change, based on values such as participation and commitment) and *ability to change* (ability to change, based on values such as flexibility and adaptation). These three intermediary factors of the change process are effectively embedded in the digital leadership approach presented below.

4.3.3 Towards a Sustainable Framework for Digital Leadership

The digital transformation framework summarises four interconnected phases that are part of an interactive feedback loop: (1) pre-phase: initiating and identifying the need for change, (2) digital strategy development (e.g. conceptualisation and goal setting), (3) transformation process (e.g. mobilisation of staff, implementation through project and quality management, personal development, implementation of results) and (4) monitoring and optimisation (see Fig. 4.2).

4.3 Digital Leadership

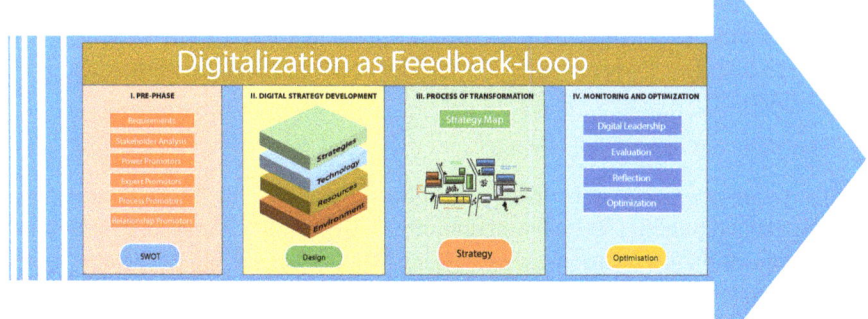

Fig. 4.2 Digital transformation framework. (Reprinted from Arnold, 2022b, licenced under CC BY 4.0)

I. Pre-Phase: Innovation in Education and Social Services Institutions

Change management is seen as a purposeful activity aimed at realising organisational change, for example, by developing and transforming strategies, processes, structures, organisational culture and external relationships. As funds, time and staff are limited and frequently insufficient in the majority of institutions, the success of digital transformation activities depends on the cooperative actions and attitudes of employees as well as the organisational innovation climate. In this preliminary phase, the requirements for the planned transformation process must therefore be analysed and defined, such as goals, organisational context, resources and barriers to innovation as well as digital competence and leadership. In addition, a stakeholder analysis assists in identifying and grouping the stakeholders to be involved in the process, according to their level of involvement, expertise, interest and influence.

Within organisations, individuals or groups in various roles actively promote and generally support innovation and change processes (Rost et al., 2007, pp. 342–343):

1. *Power promoters*, who promote innovation through hierarchical power and their connection to the company owner.
2. *Expert promoters*, who promote innovation because of their specific expertise, ideas and knowledge.
3. *Process promoters*, who have technological and organisational knowledge, are "translators" within the organisation and can bring the two aforementioned promoters together. As technological gatekeepers and due to their expert knowledge, they provide interpretation of technical information, opinion leadership.
4. *Relationship promoters*, who support the innovation process through their network competence. They are indispensable for coordination tasks, information exchange, connecting the organisation with external partners to improve relations, overcoming mistrust and settling conflicts.

All promoters described above are key actors in the innovation and transformation processes and must fulfil the expectations placed on them for successful transformation processes. They have to deal with the ignorance, unwillingness and resistance of critics ("opponents") that prevent or delay innovation processes (Rost et al., 2007).

II. *Development of a Digital Strategy*

The strategy process is the focus of the second phase of the transformation process. Euler and Seufert (2005) have established a sustainable framework for innovation in educational institutions, which understands organisations as social systems of professionals and clients. Members of the organisation behave autonomously and are challenged by the demand for self-organisation, such as self-regulated, team-based learning placed amid a constantly changing organisational culture (Arnold, 2021, p. 64). The model integrates the context and conditions ("design conditions", e.g. didactic concepts, structures, the heritage of the institution, personality and knowledge of the participants, competition, laws), the dimensions and variables of the organisation ("design variables", e.g. sustainability dimensions and factors) and strategies ("design goals", different levels of sustainability, e.g. in the form of projects, system-oriented and innovation potentials). Additionally, the authors state: "With regard to the design conditions, the environment of the university (e.g., the political system, competitive situation, legal autonomy), characteristics of the university itself (e.g., size of the university, tradition, university culture) as well as the characteristics, habits and behaviour of those involved (lecturers, students), can be distinguished" (Euler & Seufert, 2005, pp. 7–8; transl. MA). The five implementation variables developed by Euler and Seufert (2005) can be grouped into four dimensions: "(1) Change Strategies: What are the outcomes and objectives to be achieved in the process? (2) Technology: What problem-oriented infrastructure and digital learning environment do exist within the organization? (2) Resources: What support structures, processes, knowledge, communication, finances, personnel do exist within the organization? (3) Sociocultural Environment: What changes apply to individuals? Does the change process fit the socio-cultural environment? What cultural differences and health conditions should be taken into consideration?" (Arnold, 2021, p. 65).

III. *Process of Transformation: New Learning and New Work*

Phase three integrates work system theory (Alter, 2013, p. 75), which is applied generally to social and educational institutions as follows. This theory was developed to serve as a guidance and orientation system within which participants (e.g. educators, administrators, facility managers) carry out *processes and activities* (e.g. pedagogy, social work, counselling, mentoring) using *information* (e.g. organisational history, job descriptions, schedules), *technologies* (e.g. instructional approaches, digital equipment) and other *resources* (internal) to create *products/ services* (e.g. study programmes, extracurricular activities, counselling work) for specific *clients* (internal/external; e.g. customers, students, learners, service recipients) and that depend on *systemic environmental factors* (e.g. organisational,

4.3 Digital Leadership

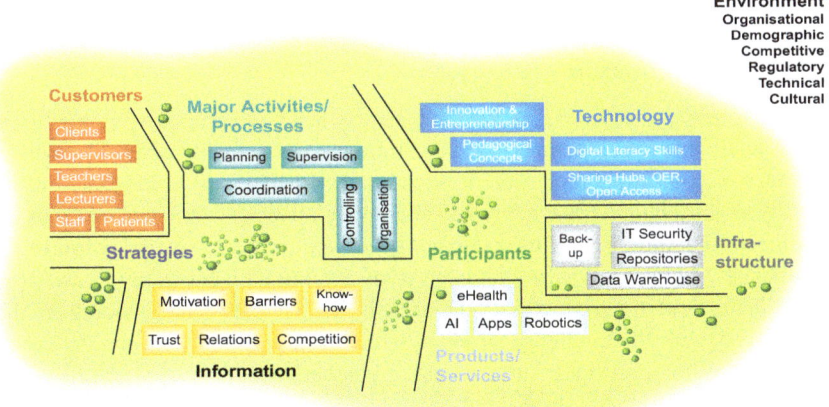

Fig. 4.3 Road map for digital leadership using the example of an educational institution. (Reprinted from Arnold, 2022c, licenced under CC BY 4.0)

sociocultural, competitive, technological, regulatory, demographic), require *infrastructure* (e.g. technical infrastructure, cloud systems jointly used with other work systems) and use *strategies* (e.g. departmental, corporate strategies). As shown in Fig. 4.3, all these factors should be aligned in the work system.

IV. Monitoring and Optimisation

The fourth phase includes different types of monitoring and further development of organisational change: *Optimisation* involves evolutionary and incremental changes of the individual parts of an organisation for fine-tuning. It can however also mean the renewal of processes that can lead to serious changes experienced as disruptions, e.g. through the introduction of new educational and support technologies. *Evaluation* is the systematic, criteria-oriented and methodically controlled process of assessing the efficiency and effectiveness, the quality, the benefits and the costs of the programmes and products provided by the organisation. Digital leadership, as a long-term view that leverages existing resources to enhance and execute anticipatory change within an organisation's culture, seeks to establish digital competencies on the basis of which future concepts may be implemented and developed in the long term.

This framework is applicable at the level of individual change agents (e.g. the various promoters), change programmes and initiatives (e.g. changes in the working environment) and the organisation as a whole. Future studies must examine the disadvantages of organisational changes and potential implementation issues (e.g. resistance and workforce barriers) (Arnold, 2021, p. 68).

4.4 Agile Leadership[3]

4.4.1 Introduction

For social work and human service institutions to sustainably assert themselves in the face of constant competition on social markets, they will need leaders with the ability to act flexibly, proactively and adaptively under dynamic and complex environmental conditions. *Agile leadership* offers a comprehensive response to these challenges, which need to be addressed when dealing with uncertainties and insecurities in the field of social work. Agile organisations in the social economy are therefore faced with the challenge of always finding an optimal balance between the transformation of services with the help of innovative management practices on the one hand and the standardisation of strategies, structures and processes on the other. In order to meet the challenges of everyday life, agile leaders must be able not only to take on different roles in a team (e.g. as mentors and decision-makers) with the help of agile methods, but agile principles should be embedded in the organisation's "operating system".

Against this background, the question arises as to what extent the practice of agile leadership can be successfully implemented in the management of social work institutions and how possible pitfalls in the practice of agile leadership can be eliminated. To answer this question and to consider the future design of leadership and collaboration in social organisations, this section is structured as follows: Firstly, the practice of agile leadership and its implementation in social work organisations is presented as a specific manifestation of the new leadership approaches in terms of transformational leadership (cf. Lippold, 2019, pp. 30, 33–34). Secondly, possible pitfalls on the implementation of agile leadership practice and leadership culture will be discussed.

4.4.2 Agile Leadership in Social Work Organisations

Agile leadership is a special form of shared leadership (cf. Pearce & Conger, 2002; Pearce & Sims, 2001, 2002) and closely related to agile project management (e.g. Highsmith, 2009), consistently oriented towards the knowledge and competences of the employees and understood as value- and principle-driven leadership. Systemically speaking, agility represents the efficiency with which organisations respond to continuous change by consistently adapting (cf. Haneberg, 2011, p. 5). Attar and Abdul-Kareem (2020, p. 173) add that agile leadership is basically a leadership concept that sees continuous adaptation to changes in the system environment, which today are characterised by increasing uncertainty, complexity and

---

[3] The following discussion of the agile leadership approach has been developed and updated based on a previous publication (Arnold, 2022d).

4.4 Agile Leadership

ambiguity, as the initial condition for management action. Agile action thus represents a readiness to act in response to (un)anticipated needs for change. It represents a management style that contributes to securing the existence of organisations. The focus is on the following basic assumptions:

1. *Levels*: Agility includes levels of values and principles,[4] methods (e.g. Scrum, Kanban, Design Thinking, Prototyping) as well as practices, techniques and tools (cf. Lippold, 2019, p. 33). The so-called AGIL scheme was introduced in the 1950s, primarily by the sociologist Talcott Parsons as part of his theory of action, as a four-phase model "adaptation", "goal attainment", "integration" and "latent pattern maintenance". According to the *Agile Manifesto*, agility is associated with the following ideas, among others: "people and interactions before processes and tools; functioning products before comprehensive documentation; collaboration with the customer before contract negotiations; and embracing change before rigid adherence to plans" (Häusling & Rutz, 2017, p. 109, transl. MA).

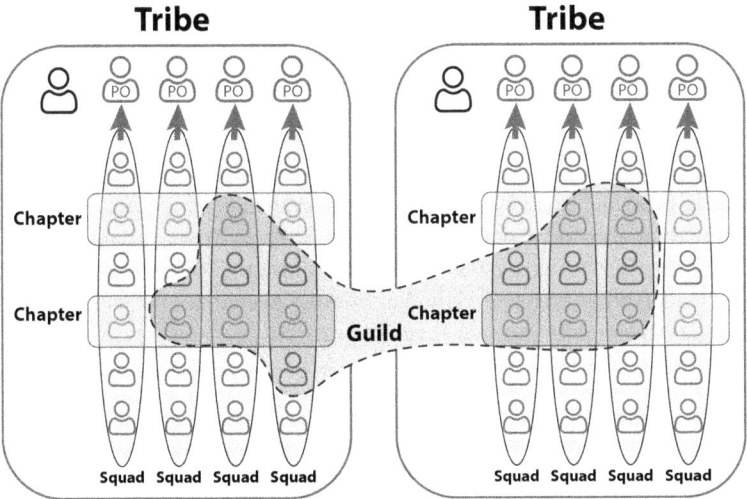

Fig. 4.4 Scaling of an agile organisation. (after Kniberg & Invarsson, 2012, p. 1, as cited in Kniberg, 2012. Used with permission)

---

[4] In particular, the following are important agile principles: "Customer satisfaction is the focus, flexible processes use change for the competitive advantage of customers, results are regularly delivered within short time spans (a few weeks or months), all participants in a project work together cooperatively on a daily basis, motivated employees are given all the resources necessary to complete the task, information transfer takes place in direct conversation as far as possible, the most important measure of progress is the functionality of the product, an even pace of work is maintained by all participants for sustainable development, the constant focus is on excellence, simplicity is essential (KISS principle), teams self-reflect on their behaviour and organisation" (Häusling & Rutz, 2017, pp. 109–110, transl. MA).

2. *Process character*: Agility requires "replacing rigid planning with lean, manageable planning and implementation cycles with concrete results and working interdisciplinarily in short iterations to be able to act and react quickly" (von Au, 2016, p. 28, transl. MA).
3. *Agile organisations are characterised in particular by flexible teamwork (see Fig. 4.4)*, which can be characterised by interdisciplinary project teams (squads) led by a product owner, cross-departmental operational knowledge work according to key topics by employees from different squads (chapters) and by cooperation between squads with a common task (tribes). Agile leadership is exercised by the product owners (process owners for their respective squad), the chapter leaders (staff managers for the chapters) and tribe leaders (managers for the overall team of the tribe) (cf. Lippold, 2019, p. 34). In other words, vertical company structures must be transformed into value chains and services.
4. *Implementation*: Employees implement their tasks in a self-determined way and are actively involved in decisions. Agility – in contrast to traditional approaches that rely on leadership and cooperation outside the team – is based on a kind of "implicit leadership" that enables intensive knowledge exchange, requires consensual action, delegates responsibility and creates a productive working environment in which all employees continuously expand, improve and renew individual and organisational knowledge stocks (e.g. Theobald et al., 2020, p. 21).

In social organisations that provide professional support and counselling services to various stakeholders, little attention has so far been given to agile leadership and its potentially positive impact on the achievement of set goals (e.g. Haworth et al., 2018). Social workers tend to adopt a systemic perspective when seeking solutions to complex social person-centred service provision and a relational leadership style (see Adams et al., 2013; Rank & Hutchison, 2000).

Agile leadership in social work organisations – even if not yet widely practiced – offers extensions of previous management practices in many ways (Arnold, 2022a, p. 131):

Consistent Focus on Effective Teamwork. "Social person-related services" (Klatetzki, 2010, p. 8) are usually provided as a team effort or are more often co-produced by professionals and clients. According to Morrison et al. (2019, pp. 117–124), agile leadership contributes significantly to the implementation of teamwork in the organisation. In contrast to individual performance, working in a team typically leads to faster and more successful achievement of set goals or implementation of upcoming tasks. An agile leader is therefore responsible for creating a productive working environment for the team, in which the necessary roles are distributed, and responsibilities delegated.

Continuous Learning and Optimisation. Agile leadership means undergoing a continuous learning process in joint work and striving for regular improvement. In social work, this requires leaders to have emotional intelligence and cultural competence in addition to all professional and methodological skills and abilities. Leaders should also have various personal competences that enable them to reflect on their own actions, thoughts, feelings and values, as well as those of others, and to change perspectives. Continuously learning from one's own strengths and weaknesses is an attitude that the agile leader must also establish.

Increasing the Commitment, Self-Responsibility and Self-Organisation of Employees. Agile leadership is particularly necessary in social institutions that provide physically and mentally demanding services. Breakspear (2017) argues that agile leadership can increase the motivation and commitment of employees if they are directly involved in decision-making processes and are thus more closely tied to the implementation of organisational goals and tasks. It is also important that tasks and processes are implemented in self-organised teams. In this way, employees have a greater sense of being taken seriously and can also increase their responsibility in and for the organisation as well as for themselves. Staff as well as volunteers are thus more engaged and can directly address the challenges they face in their work.

Agile Leadership Only Works in a Culture of Trust. According to Brandes et al. (2014, p. 98), various aspects and factors are decisive for the further development of organisational culture: "The image of man is decisive here, because all other values can be inferred almost automatically on this basis: If the image of man in a company is characterised by the will to work creatively and productively, by self-organisation, passion and respect, clarity, open mutual feedback, courage to engage in difficult discussions and general transparent communication at eye level are not far away" (Häusling & Rutz, 2017, pp. 114–115; transl. MA). This is because agile management within organisations requires a shift of responsibility and decision-making power towards self-determined work and employees' personal responsibility for the social and personal services offered.

In summary, these studies show that the integration of agile leadership principles in social work organisations can be helpful in terms of the effectiveness of teamwork, continuous learning of managers and staff and overcoming the challenges faced by staff and volunteers. Nevertheless, agile leadership approaches have been criticised as well as praised in the academic debate. The prevailing opinion is that agile methods are very well accepted in practice and offer particular advantages in project work (e.g. Highsmith, 2009). Similarly, individual empirical studies confirm that agile approaches are slightly less "enthusiastically" used in many companies than reported in earlier studies (cf. Komus & Kuberg, 2017, pp. 3–5; Spiegler et al., 2021). The positive effects cited by users of agile leadership principles include faster project development, quality assurance and risk diversification (Komus & Kuberg, 2017). In particular, embedding the agile approach in the organisational strategy, structure as well as culture and the implementation of suitable agile methods, the transfer of responsibility to the team and flexible staff development methods are seen as necessary prerequisites or conditions for the success of agile leadership (cf. Lippold, 2019, pp. 33–34). In the context of the influence of agile working methods on administrative social work practices in the field of child protection, it was found that social workers in these working contexts have less privacy and space for themselves. Especially when it comes to complicated decisions, agile working structures tend to cause interruptions in thinking processes rather than leading to more effective collaboration or better quality decisions; however, there is also evidence that agile working is associated with joy, usefulness and freedom (cf. Jeyasingham, 2019, p. 572). Empirical studies investigating the influence of agile working methods in social work are generally scarce (e.g. Jeyasingham, 2016, 2020).

4.4.3 Challenges for the Implementation of Agile Leadership Practices in Social Work Organisations

Considering the advantages and disadvantages of the use of agile leadership in social work institutions, the following section discusses potential barriers as well as possible solutions and conditions for success when implementing agile leadership in practice (cf. Table 4.1). The solutions presented should not be misunderstood as a "panacea", but show that in the practice of agile leadership, it is not or cannot be a matter of simply implementing newly learned methods (e.g. Design Thinking, Kanban, Prototyping, Scrum). Rather, many other (hard and soft) factors are involved in determining whether one's own institution can be transformed into an agile organisation.

The transformation to an agile business model can be implemented, mainly by using the following three essential components (Fig. 4.5): The objective formulation, design and prototyping of the new agile business model take place within the context of a design thinking process. After *describing the problem* based on a needs and situation analysis, an *agile solution* is created, developed as a *prototype* by one or more agile teams and then *evaluated or optimised*. These sub-steps are believed to be components of an iterative process in which explicit backtracking is sought. Furthermore, new work structures and roles must be developed, assigned and modified. This may be accomplished by utilising Kniberg's (2012) agile system structure, which was described in depth in Sect. 4.4.2 (see Fig. 4.4) (3). Lastly, the newly discovered agile structures and processes must be scaled and constantly refined during the agile transformation process. This will result in a transformation of the organisation's identity; managers and staff must be supported consistently in building their skills and resources (e.g. staff development measures, changes in decision-making processes, transfer of responsibility, provision of material, human and financial resources). In order for the agile transformation to succeed, two prerequisites must be clarified: Firstly, continuous testing, an active learning culture and a willingness to change must be promoted. Secondly, coordination and communication in the form of a change team, responsible for addressing the various challenges in agile transformation, is essential for shaping the organisational change process (cf. Table 4.1).

Table 4.1 Stumbling blocks and solutions for agile leadership (author's own illustration)

Stumbling blocks	Approaches
Insufficient anchoring of agile principles in corporate and leadership culture	In order to achieve the "mindshift" towards agile management practice, managers must be empowered in agile principles and methods, and their courage to change must be actively promoted. Agile leadership requires, for example, an appreciative error culture and open feedback
Leadership is understood as management and not leadership	Agile leadership is not about a specific organisational competence. In practice, it is much more important to create space that motivates the development of new offers and the realisation of visions, to continuously question or challenge the status quo, to involve all stakeholders in strategic leadership actions and to live trust
Agile management is attempted to be transferred to the entire institution	Certainly, the implementation of agile principles and methods starts with the management team but does not have to be implemented across the board in the entire organisation. The integration of agile approaches makes more sense in areas that are characterised by change and project work and where networked solutions are important
Agile management principles can be implemented project-like and across the board in the company	The agile transformation will only succeed if employees have not only developed an understanding of the agile mindset but are also prepared to consistently align all services with the needs of clients and other stakeholders. The introduction of an agile management approach is not a project, but a continuous change process
Implementation simply needs to be ordered by top management	In practice, it is advisable not to introduce agile management practices without offering reflection and supervision. External coaches can support in the correct execution of agile methods. Regular collegial reflection and supervision are recommended for managers
With the elimination of hierarchies, there is a gap in communication and decision-making structures	It is advisable to communicate guiding objectives when introducing agile leadership practices (cf. principles for change management according to Kotter (1995)) and to prevent employees from falling back into old behavioural patterns

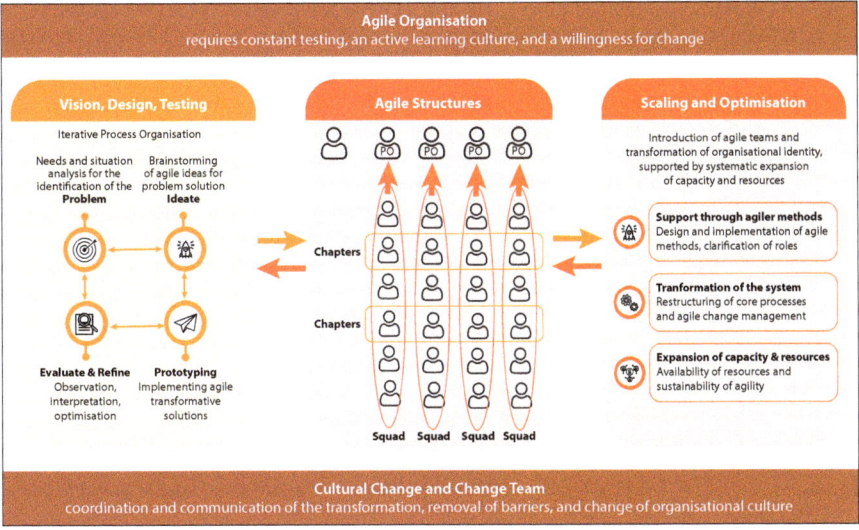

Fig. 4.5 Process of agile transformation. (own representation based on Kniberg, 2012 and Brosseau et al., 2019. Used with permission)

References

Adams, J. A., Bailey, D. E., Jr., Anderson, R. A., & Thygeson, M. (2013). Finding your way through EOL challenges in the ICU using adaptive leadership behaviours. *Intensive and Critical Care Nursing, 29*(6), 329–336. https://doi.org/10.1016/j.iccn.2013.05.004

Alter, S. (2013). Work system theory: Overview of core concepts, extensions, and challenges for the future. *Journal of the Association for Information Systems, 14*(2), 72–121. https://doi.org/10.17705/1jais.00323

Arnold, M. (2019). Leading change in human service organisations in the 21st century. In M. W. Fröse, B. Naake, & M. Arnold (Eds.), *Führung und organisation: Neue Entwicklungen im management der Sozial- und Gesundheitswirtschaft* (pp. 159–174). Springer. https://doi.org/10.1007/978-3-658-24193-3_8

Arnold, M. (2020). Leading digital change – Management of Hybridity and Change in education and social service institutions. In T. Koehler, E. Schoop, & N. Kahnwald (Eds.), Gemeinschaften in Neuen Medien. *Von hybriden Realitäten zu hybriden Gemeinschaften. Proceedings of 23nd Conference GeNeMe 2020* (pp. 332–341). TUDpress. https://nbn-resolving.org/urn:nbn:de:bsz:14-qucosa2-741338

Arnold, M. (2021). Leading digital change and the Management of Hybridity in social work organizations. In F. Özsungur (Ed.), *Handbook of research on policies, protocols, and practices for social work in the digital world* (pp. 55–73). IGI Global. https://doi.org/10.4018/978-1-7998-7772-1.ch004

Arnold, M. (2022a). Agiles Führen und Managen in der Sozialen Arbeit: Stolpersteine auf dem Weg zur agilen Führungspraxis. In J. Grothe (Ed.), *Leitung, Führung und management in der Sozialen Arbeit: Bedeutungshorizonte und Konzepte auf dem Prüfstand* (pp. 123–138). Beltz Juventa.

Arnold, M. (2022b). *Digital transformation framework* (Version1). [figshare]. https://doi.org/10.6084/m9.figshare.20079932.v1.

Arnold, M. (2022c). *Road map for digital leadership* (Version1). [figshare]. https://doi.org/10.6084/m9.figshare.20079962.v1.

Arnold, M. (2022d). A Short History of Management Thought. In M. Arnold (Ed.), *Grundlagen des Sozialmanagements – Ein Open Educational Textbook*. https://doi.org/10.21428/5ecaacfc.ec0e3c01

Attar, M., & Abdul-Kareem, A. (2020). The role of agile leadership in organisational agility. In B. Akkaya (Ed.), *Agile business leadership methods for industry 4.0* (pp. 171–191). Emerald Publishing. https://doi.org/10.1108/9781800433809

Bowersox, D. J., Closs, D. J., & Drayer, R. W. (2005). The digital transformation: Technology and beyond. *Supply Chain Management Review, 9*(1), 22–29.

Brandes, U., Gemmer, P., Koschek, H., & Schültken, L. (2014). *Management Y. Agile, scrum, Design Thinking & Co.: So gelingt der Wandel zur attraktiven und zukunftsfähigen organisation*. Campus.

Breakspear, S. (2017). Embracing agile leadership for learning: How leaders can create impact despite growing complexity. *Australian Educational Leader, 39*(3), 68–71.

Brennen, J. S., & Kreiss, D. (2016). Digitalization. In K. B. Jensen, E. W. Rothenbuhler, J. D. Pooley, & R. T. Craig (Eds.), *The international encyclopedia of communication theory and philosophy* (pp. 1–11). Wiley. https://doi.org/10.1002/9781118766804.wbiect111

Brosseau, D., Ebrahim, S., Handscomb, C., & Thaker, S. (2019, May 10). *The journey to an agile organization. McKinsey & Company*. [Blog]. https://www.mckinsey.com/business-functions/organization/our-insights/the-journey-to-an-agile-organization#

Burnes, B. (2004). Kurt Lewin and the planned approach to change: A re-appraisal. *Journal of Management Studies, 41*(6), 977–1002. https://doi.org/10.1111/j.1467-6486.2004.00463.x

Douse, M., & Uys, P. (2018). Educational planning in the age of digitisation. *Educational Planning, 25*(2), 7–23.

Dugan, J. P. (2017). *Leadership theory: Cultivating critical perspectives*. John Wiley & Sons.

References

Euler, D., & Seufert, S. (2005). Change management in der Hochschullehre: Die nachhaltige Implementierung von e-learning-Innovationen. *Zeitschrift für Hochschulentwicklung, 3*, 3–15. https://www.zfhe.at/index.php/zfhe/article/view/187/314

Grodsky, T. (n.d.). *History of management thought*. http://faculty.wwu.edu/dunnc3/rprnts.historyofmanagementthought.pdf

Hall, R., Atkins, L., & Fraser, J. (2014). Defining a self-evaluation digital literacy framework for secondary educators: The DigiLit Leicester project. *Research in Learning Technology, 22*, 1–17. https://doi.org/10.3402/rlt.v22.21440

Haneberg, L. (2011). Training for agility: Building the skills employees need to zig and Zag. *Human Resource Management International Digest, 20*(2), 50–58.

Häusling, A., & Rutz, B. (2017). Agile Führungsstrukturen und Führungskulturen zur Förderung der Selbstorganisation – Ausgestaltung und Herausforderungen. In C. von Au (Ed.), *Struktur und Kultur einer leadership-organisation: Leadership und Angewandte Psychologie* (Vol. Bd. 2, pp. 105–122). Springer. https://doi.org/10.1007/978-3-658-12554-7_6

Haworth, S., Miller, R., & Schaub, J. (2018). *Leadership in social work: (and can it learn from clinical healthcare?)*. University of Birmingham. https://www.birmingham.ac.uk/Documents/college-social-sciences/social-policy/Misc/leadership-in-social-work.pdf

Heifetz, R. A. (1994). *Leadership without easy answers*. Belknap Press.

Heifetz, R. A., Grashow, A., & Linsky, M. (2009). *The practice of adaptive leadership: Tools and tactics for changing your organisation and the world*. Harvard Business Press.

Highsmith, J. A. (2009). *Agile Project Management: Creating innovative products* (1st ed.). Pearson Education.

Jeyasingham, D. (2016). Open spaces, supple bodies? Considering the impact of agile working on social work office practices. *Child & Family Social Work, 21*(2), 209–217. https://doi.org/10.1111/cfs.12130

Jeyasingham, D. (2019). Seeking solitude and distance from others: Children's social workers' agile working practices and experiences beyond the office. *The British Journal of Social Work, 49*(3), 559–576. https://doi.org/10.1093/bjsw/bcy077

Jeyasingham, D. (2020). Entanglements with offices, information systems, laptops and phones: How agile working is influencing social workers' interactions with each other and with families. *Qualitative Social Work, 19*(3), 337–358. https://doi.org/10.1177/1473325020911697

Khalid, J., Ram, B. R., Soliman, M., Ali, A. J., Khaleel, M., & Islam, M. S. (2018). Promising digital university: A pivotal need for higher education transformation. *International Journal of Management in Education, 12*(3), 264–275.

Klatetzki, T. (2010). Zur Einführung: Soziale personenbezogene Dienstleistungsorganisation als Typus. In T. Klatetzki (Ed.), *Soziale personenbezogene Dienstleistungsorganisationen: Soziologische Perspektiven* (pp. 7–24). Springer VS. https://doi.org/10.1007/978-3-531-92474-8_1

Kniberg, H. (2012, November 14). Scaling agile @ Spotify with tribes, squads, Chapters & Guilds. *crisp* [Blog]. https://blog.crisp.se/2012/11/14/henrikkniberg/scaling-agile-at-spotify

Komus, A., & Kuberg, M. (2017). *Status Quo Agile: Studie zu Verbreitung und Nutzen agiler Methoden. Eine empirische Untersuchung*. GPM Deutsche Gesellschaft für Projektmanagement e. V.

Kotter, J. P. (1995). Leading change: Why transformation efforts fail. *Harvard Business Review, 73*(2), 59–67.

Kreidenweis, H. (2018). Sozialwirtschaft im digitalen Wandel. In H. Kreidenweis (Ed.), *Digitaler Wandel in der Sozialwirtschaft* (pp. 9–26). Nomos.

Kreutzer, R. T., Neugebauer, T., & Pattloch, A. (2018). *Digital business leadership: Digital transformation, business model innovation, agile organization, change management*. Springer Gabler. https://doi.org/10.1007/978-3-662-56548-3

Krüger, W. (2009). *Excellence in change: Wege Zur Strategischen Erneuerung* (4th ed.). Gabler. https://doi.org/10.1007/978-3-8349-4717-8

Lippold, D. (2019). *Führungskultur im Wandel: Klassische und moderne Führungsansätze im Zeitalter der Digitalisierung*. Springer Gabler. https://doi.org/10.1007/978-3-658-25855-9

Mack, O., Khare, A., Krämer, A., & Burgartz, T. (Eds.). (2015). *Managing in a VUCA world*. Springer. https://doi.org/10.1007/978-3-319-16889-0

Morrison, E., Hutcheson, S., Nilsen, E., Fadden, J., & Franklin, N. (2019). *Strategic doing: Ten skills for agile leadership*. Wiley.

Nelson, T., & Squires, V. (2017). Addressing complex challenges through adaptive leadership: A promising approach to collaborative problem solving. *Journal of Leadership Education, 16*(4), 111–123. https://doi.org/10.12806/V16/I4/T2

Northouse, P. G. (2016). Leadership: Theory and practice. In *Leadership theory and practice* (7th Edn.). SAGE.

Orlikowski, W. J. (1996). Improvising organizational transformation over time: A situated change perspective. *Information Systems Research, 7*(1), 63–92. https://doi.org/10.1287/isre.7.1.63

Pearce, C. L., & Conger, J. A. (2002). *Shared leadership: Reframing the hows and whys of leadership*. SAGE. https://doi.org/10.4135/9781452229539

Pearce, C. L., & Sims, H. P. (2001). Shared leadership: Toward a multi-level theory of leadership. *Advances in Interdisciplinary Studies of Work Teams, 7*, 115–139. https://doi.org/10.1016/S1572-0977(00)07008-4

Pearce, C. L., & Sims, H. P. (2002). Vertical versus shared leadership as predictors of the effectiveness of change management teams: An examination of aversive, directive, transactional, transformational, and empowering leader behaviors. *Group Dynamics, 6*, 172–197. https://doi.org/10.1037//1089-2699.6.2.172

Porras, J. I., & Silvers, R. C. (1991). Organisation development and transformation. *Annual Review of Psychology, 42*, 51–78. https://doi.org/10.1146/annurev.ps.42.020191.000411

Rank, M. G., & Hutchison, W. S. (2000). An analysis of leadership within the social work profession. *Journal of Social Work Education, 36*(3), 487–502. https://doi.org/10.1080/10437797.2000.10779024

Rost, K., Hölzle, K., & Gemünden, H. G. (2007). Promotors or champions? Pros and cons of role specialisation for economic process. *Schmalenbach Business Review, 59*(4), 340–363. https://doi.org/10.5167/uzh-68489

Sheninger, E. (2019). *Digital leadership: Changing paradigms for changing times*. Corwin Press.

Spiegler, S. V., Heinecke, C., & Wagner, S. (2021). An empirical study on changing leadership in agile teams. *Empirical Software Engineering, 26*, 41. https://doi.org/10.1007/s10664-021-09949-5

Theobald, S., Prenner, N., Krieg, A., & Schneider, K. (2020). Agile leadership and agile management on organizational level-a systematic literature review. In M. Morisio, M. Torchiano, & A. Jedlitschka (Eds.), *International conference on product-focused software process improvement: 21st international conference, PROFES 2020 proceedings* (pp. 20–36). Springer. https://doi.org/10.1007/978-3-030-64148-1_2

Uhl-Bien, M., Marion, R., & McKelvey, B. (2007). Complexity leadership theory: Shifting leadership from the industrial age to the knowledge era. *Leadership Quarterly, 18*, 298–318. https://doi.org/10.1016/j.leaqua.2007.04.002

Von Au, C. (2016). Paradigmenwechsel in der Führung: Traditionelle Führungsansätze, Wandel und leadership heute. In C. von Au (Ed.), *Wirksame und nachhaltige Führungsansätze: System, Beziehung, Haltung und Individualität* (pp. 1–42). Springer. https://doi.org/10.1007/978-3-658-11956-0_1

Weick, K. E., & Quinn, R. E. (1999). Organizational change and development. *Annual Review of Psychology, 50*, 361–386. https://doi.org/10.1146/annurev.psych.50.1.361

Chapter 5
Conclusion and Outlook

5.1　Implications for Leadership and Collaboration in Social Work Organisations

As shown above, *adaptive leadership* and *digital leadership* competencies are key to achieving change in any organisation. Both models provide new insights into how leadership can be implemented in social work organisations, e.g. by regularly reflecting one's own leadership practice, i.e. "to get on the balcony", by guiding people and teams instead of directing them, by creating an active learning climate, by establishing stability, by clearly communicating strategic goals, by developing digital competences and by sustainably shaping digital change management (Heifetz et al., 2009). Further research is needed to better understand the theoretical underpinnings of the relationships between the different challenges, leadership behaviour and adaptive or digital work.

Leadership agility may be regarded as a reaction to a social work organisation's environment that is becoming increasingly complex, unpredictable and dynamic. Social and human service organisations must continually adapt to changing market conditions in a dynamic and timely manner. As noted before, agile leadership structures also necessitate the incorporation of new values into the organisational culture, a shift in client and employee focus as well as the creation, testing and evaluation of agile leadership methods and procedures. Integration of agile concepts into an organisation's culture is sometimes difficult, since all management and leadership actions must now be viewed as a service to workers. This necessitates that managers present themselves less as doers or specialists and more as systematically active, motivating coaches in daily life.

This aspect is also related with a rethinking of the use of other and in part new human resource management instruments, which enable co-creation, among other things. Sprints, design thinking and prototyping approaches can be used to develop an agile mindset among all members of the organisation, but this requires a different feedback culture (characterised by 360° feedback via stand-ups, reviews, sprints, portfolios and target agreements). Further key components for establishing an agile mindset include an agile organisational structure (with recourse to decentralised organisational structures such as socio−/holacracy; cf. Schell & Bischof, 2022) and the combination of the client value orientation with the individual contribution orientation. Those who advocate for greater agility must also create a productive work environment where disagreements and conflicts can be resolved in a goal-oriented manner and where there is open communication, transparency and a "forward-open" error culture as well as cross-departmental and cross-professional cooperation.

Agile leadership in social organisations is successful when, for example, the leadership practice is regularly reflected and the focus is on guiding and supporting people and teams instead of directing them, and strategic goals are clearly communicated (cf. Arnold, 2019, p. 169). The theoretical underpinnings of the links between the numerous issues, leadership behaviour and agile practise require more research in the future. It may be difficult to impose an unequivocal rejection of agile ideas and processes; even sceptics tend to rate them highly, despite being concerned more often about possible negative effects (cf. Jeyasingham, 2019, p. 572). In circumstances when reaching a goal may be in conflict with the organisation's values or its own ideas and principles, it is especially crucial to consider the moral or ethical dimension (e.g. change does not always lead to improved conditions). Additional attention should be paid to the shift in the work environment observed in some areas (e.g. remote work), which is linked to qualitatively different forms of "sense of community" (cf. Weick et al., 2005) in agile organisations and the use of new technology-based media in social work (e.g. mobile devices in public spaces and domestic, private environments).

For the implementation of the aforementioned leadership models in social work organisations in general, leaders need to fulfil a number of requirements: On the one hand, relevant competencies need to be developed as part of the management education of social workers, health professionals and other specialists in academic leadership programmes at universities (Sect. 5.2). On the other hand, leaders must adhere to the principles for shaping organisational change (Sect. 5.3).

5.2 Requirements for Management Learning and Teaching in Higher Education

In order to successfully manage leadership and collaboration in organisations, leaders should always use available research, models and approaches as well as specialised coaching and consulting services to seek solutions to upcoming challenges. In staff-intensive service enterprises in the social and health economy, the quality of staff and organisational management depends to a large extent on the professional and management skills and qualifications of, among others, the employed social workers, educators, nurses and social managers (e.g. Hafford-Letchfield et al., 2014). In this respect, the various curricula of higher education programmes in the field of social work, early childhood education and care and health management also focus on the professional competencies of the respective field of work. Topics such as the introduction to the management of the social economy, stakeholder management, accounting, marketing, organisation-related management and human resource management are, however, still far too rare in the curricula. Besides, students also need to be familiarised with methods such as organisational analysis, target agreement discussions, survey techniques and action research. The development of skills and abilities in social management should also focus on analytical, empirical-methodological and reflexive competencies. In addition, continuous cooperation should be established between higher education institutions in the field of applied research and training. Higher education institutions must also align themselves with the requirements of professional practice, which is done, for example, through the development of in-service study programmes, the provision of continuing education and the development of practice within research projects. In these projects, transferable components can be developed, tested and continuously revised – among other things through service learning (cf. Arnold, 2022a).

The social economy requires an inter- and transdisciplinary approach to management. As shown in Fig. 5.1, various bachelor's, master's and doctoral programmes in social work management education must incorporate knowledge and skills from several academic disciplines, including business and economics, public management, social and human sciences, sustainability sciences, cultural sciences, etc. (cf. in more detail in Arnold, 2021).

Due to this hybrid character, it is always feasible to draw on results, learning objects and research perspectives from other academic disciplines, but it is also necessary to address the didacticisation of this work field and topic. Phase-oriented didactic planning and design includes (1) defining the *learning outcomes*, (2) identifying the learning *requirements*, (3) *didactic analysis and reduction* of the topic and (4) the selection of adequate learning and teaching methods. The last step is to assess the didactics of social management from a theoretical, methodological and practical-conceptual standpoint to identify future research and practice requirements.

5.3 Leadership and Management in Uncertain Times

Increasingly, leadership and collaboration are also challenged by the digital transformation which is affecting all areas of our lives, ultimately also in social institutions. As hybrid organisations, they not only have to mediate between the dynamics of state-based, market-based and societal structures but also take into account the different rationalities, values and interests of stakeholders. As outlined in Sect. 4.3, digital transformation in these organisations requires a sustainable human resource and organisational development process that combines four interrelated phases: (1) identification of change needs and peoples' readiness, (2) development of a digital transformation strategy, (3) implementation of the transformation and (4)

Fig. 5.1 Hybrid function of social work management education. (Reprinted from Arnold, 2022b, licenced under CC BY 4.0, adapted from Arnold, 2021, p. 57 which is based on Wöhrle, 2006, p. 113, as cited in Brinkmann, 2010, p. 25)

monitoring and optimisation. This framework can be applied at the level of individual change agents (e.g. the various promoters), change programmes and initiatives (e.g. changes in the work environment) and at the level of the organisation itself. Future research needs to further explore the organisational challenges and potential implementation issues (e.g. resistance, workforce barriers), and there is a need to promote and develop relevant digital competencies in education, training and professional development. To master these kinds of changes in social and human service organisations, a specific attitude towards social and organisational changes needs to be developed within these institutions.

In an essay on the principles of leadership in organisational change, John Kotter (1995) described eight principles that relate to the different competencies that adaptive and "digital leaders" should possess to successfully implement change in organisations. In social work organisations, according to Kotter (1995, p. 61), leaders should be able to:

- *Create a sense of urgency among all stakeholders*: a potential crisis caused by challenges within the organisational environment and the artificial maintenance of the status quo is often dangerous.
- *Build viable coalitions within and outside the organisation*: it is crucial for the change process to build heterogeneous groups of people, including staff from human resource management and quality management.
- *Develop a shared vision* that is evolvable to survive in the long term and that helps to link analytical thinking and goal development.
- *Communicate vision clearly and credibly* through all available communication channels, in word and in action.
- *Empower staff and stakeholders to act according to the organisational change vision*: we often have to acknowledge that we cannot free ourselves from all resistance. Therefore, all stakeholders involved in the process need to be treated fairly, regardless of who is resisting the changes and how.
- *Plan for and achieve short-term success*: hoping for change is not enough. Visions can be revised, adapted, refined and expanded.
- *Consolidate improvements and make the change permanent*: success can also be a threat to change. A good plan for change includes small and large milestones.
- *Institutionalise new approaches and integrate them into the organisational culture*: leaders should show staff how to implement change and how to improve the quality of results. Leaders must therefore have clear objectives.

To cultivate an adaptive culture of leadership and collaboration within an organisation, Heifetz et al. (2009, as cited in Wong & Chan, 2018) suggest some strategies in this context:

- *Making "name the elephant in the room" the norm*: identifying the challenges that everyone avoids.
- *Cultivating shared responsibility for the organisation*: all people within the organisation should have a sense of responsibility for the whole organisation.
- *Encouraging independent judgement*: each person should be mobilised and motivated to adapt their work practice in their respective roles.
- *Developing leadership capacity among organisational members*: human resource development and training of organisational culture in the workplace.
- *Institutionalising reflection and continuous learning*: constant reflection, feedback culture and experimentation should be part of every organisation.

The aforementioned principles and requirements focus directly on actors involved in managing change within a particular organisation – in other words, leadership is understood as an *activity*. Future leaders should also focus their attention more on management processes for conceptual and organisational development as well as on managing the active creation of a living (organisational) culture and strategic human resource development.

This book offers its readers various scientifically grounded perspectives, and, due to its inter–/ transdisciplinary and cross-methodological approach, it addresses not only teachers and students of social work and human service management but also experienced practitioners. It offers significant points of reflection for the further development of the respective academic field: *Firstly*, leadership in social work institutions can always be seen as relational work amid uncertainty and insecurity. Accordingly, in professional practice, attention should be paid to "questioning old certainties and further developing strategies for dealing with uncertainty and insecurity" (Effinger, 2021, p. 234; transl. MA). The aim should therefore be to instil curiosity and "theoretical doubt" in prospective students when dealing with ambivalences. *Secondly*, the book clearly demonstrates that both the formulation of goals for leadership interventions and the transfer between theory and practice require emotional anchoring and dialogue-based negotiation processes between all participants. *Thirdly*, compared to Effinger (2018), there is an expansion to include epistemological and decision-theoretical foundations of human action for a better understanding of coping with uncertainty as a key competence in social and human service organisations. Self-competence is thereby seen as an essential component in the interplay of self-awareness and self-perception, self-control, self-observation and self-regulation. To summarise, the promotion and development of this type of self-competence is a crucial future challenge in the further evolution of the academic discipline and profession of social work. *Fourthly*, it can often be observed that particularly practice reflection and supervision have increasingly developed into a place for solving business-related team and organisational development processes and conflicts caused by them. The focus of counselling and supervision should, therefore, be shifted back to the genuine professional level and the competence development of the professional actors and leadership (cf. Effinger, 2018). Finally, more studies are needed to clarify the conceptualisation of leadership as expressed in various approaches, theories and methods and to confirm the underlying assumptions and hypotheses.

References

Arnold, M. (2019). Leading change in human service Organisations in the 21st century. In M. W. Fröse, B. Naake, & M. Arnold (Eds.), *Führung und Organisation: Neue Entwicklungen im Management der Sozial- und Gesundheitswirtschaft* (pp. 159–174). Springer. https://doi.org/10.1007/978-3-658-24193-3_8

Arnold, M. (2021). Leading digital change and the Management of Hybridity in social work organizations. In F. Özsungur (Ed.), *Handbook of research on policies, protocols, and practices for social work in the digital world* (pp. 55–73). IGI Global. https://doi.org/10.4018/978-1-7998-7772-1.ch004

Arnold, M. (2022a). Problem-based learning and community engagement: A service-learning project with social pedagogues. In U. Fahr, A. Kenner, H. Angenent, & A. Eßer-Lüghausen (Eds.), *Hochschullehre erforschen: Innovative impulse für das scholarship of teaching and learning* (pp. 199–214). Springer. https://doi.org/10.1007/978-3-658-34185-5_11

Arnold, M. (2022b). *Hybrid function of social work management education* (version 1). [figshare]. https://doi.org/10.6084/m9.figshare.20079650.v1

Effinger, H. (2018). *Beratung in der Sozialwirtschaft: Ungewissheiten als Chance kreativer Problemlösungsstrategien.* Vandenhoeck & Ruprecht.

References

Effinger, H. (2021). *Soziale Arbeit im Ungewissen. Mit Selbstkompetenz aus Eindeutigkeitsfallen: Professionell erkennen, verantwortlich entscheiden und handeln*. Beltz Juventa.

Hafford-Letchfield, T., Lambley, S., Spolander, G., & Cocker, C. (2014). *Inclusive leadership in social work and social care*. Policy Press.

Heifetz, R. A., Grashow, A., & Linsky, M. (2009). *The practice of adaptive leadership: Tools and tactics for changing your organisation and the world*. Harvard Business Press.

Jeyasingham, D. (2019). Seeking solitude and distance from others: Children's social workers' agile working practices and experiences beyond the office. *The British Journal of Social Work, 49*(3), 559–576. https://doi.org/10.1093/bjsw/bcy077

Kotter, J. P. (1995). Leading change: Why transformation efforts fail. *Harvard Business Review, 73*(2), 59–67.

Schell, S., & Bischof, N. (2022). Change the way of working. Ways into self-organization with the use of Holacracy: An empirical investigation. *European Management Review, 19*(1), 123–137. https://doi.org/10.1111/emre.12457

Weick, K., Sutcliffe, K. M., & Obstfeld, D. (2005). Organizing and the process of sensemaking. *Organization Science, 16*(4), 409–421. https://doi.org/10.1287/orsc.1050.0133

Wong, G. K. W., & Chan, D. L. H. (2018). Adaptive leadership in academic libraries. *Library Management, 39*(1/2), 106–115. https://doi.org/10.1108/LM-06-2017-0060

Index

A
Adaptive leadership, 2, 37–39, 44–49, 65
Agile leadership, 1, 2, 56–61, 65, 66

C
Conclusions, 18, 39, 44, 65–70

D
Digital/virtual leadership, 2, 26, 27, 45, 50–55, 65
Dimensions, 2, 13, 15, 16, 18–20, 22, 33, 34, 39, 49, 54, 66

H
Higher education, 66, 67

I
Introduction, 1–2, 23, 52, 55, 56, 61, 67

L
Leadership, 1, 2, 5–28, 33–39, 43–61, 65–70
Leadership challenges, 48, 50
Leadership research, 6, 13, 33–39

M
Management, 1, 2, 5–11, 14, 15, 21, 25–27, 34–36, 38, 39, 43–46, 50, 52, 53, 56–59, 61, 65–67, 69, 70
Management learning, 66, 67

N
New leadership approaches, 11, 19–22, 56

S
Systemic approaches, 36, 39

T
Transformational leadership, 11, 14, 20, 23, 56

U
Uncertainty, 47, 56, 70

GPSR Compliance

The European Union's (EU) General Product Safety Regulation (GPSR) is a set of rules that requires consumer products to be safe and our obligations to ensure this.

If you have any concerns about our products, you can contact us on

ProductSafety@springernature.com

In case Publisher is established outside the EU, the EU authorized representative is:

Springer Nature Customer Service Center GmbH
Europaplatz 3
69115 Heidelberg, Germany

www.ingramcontent.com/pod-product-compliance
Ingram Content Group UK Ltd.
Pitfield, Milton Keynes, MK11 3LW, UK
UKHW021254180426
11947UKWH00010B/781